SHORT CUT TO NIRVANA

JANE COMER

For current news on Tibet
go to
www.phayul.com

Copyright © 2012 by Jane Comer. 700274-COMB
ISBN: Softcover 978-1-4691-5792-4

All rights reserved. No part of this book may be reproduced or transmitted in any form or by any means, electronic or mechanical, including photocopying, recording, or by any information storage and retrieval system, without permission in writing from the copyright owner.

This is a work of non fiction. Some of the people in this book may have had their names changed to protect their identities.

This book was printed in the United States of America.

To order additional copies of this book, contact:
Xlibris Corporation
0800-891-366
www.xlibris.co.nz
Orders@ Xlibris.co.nz

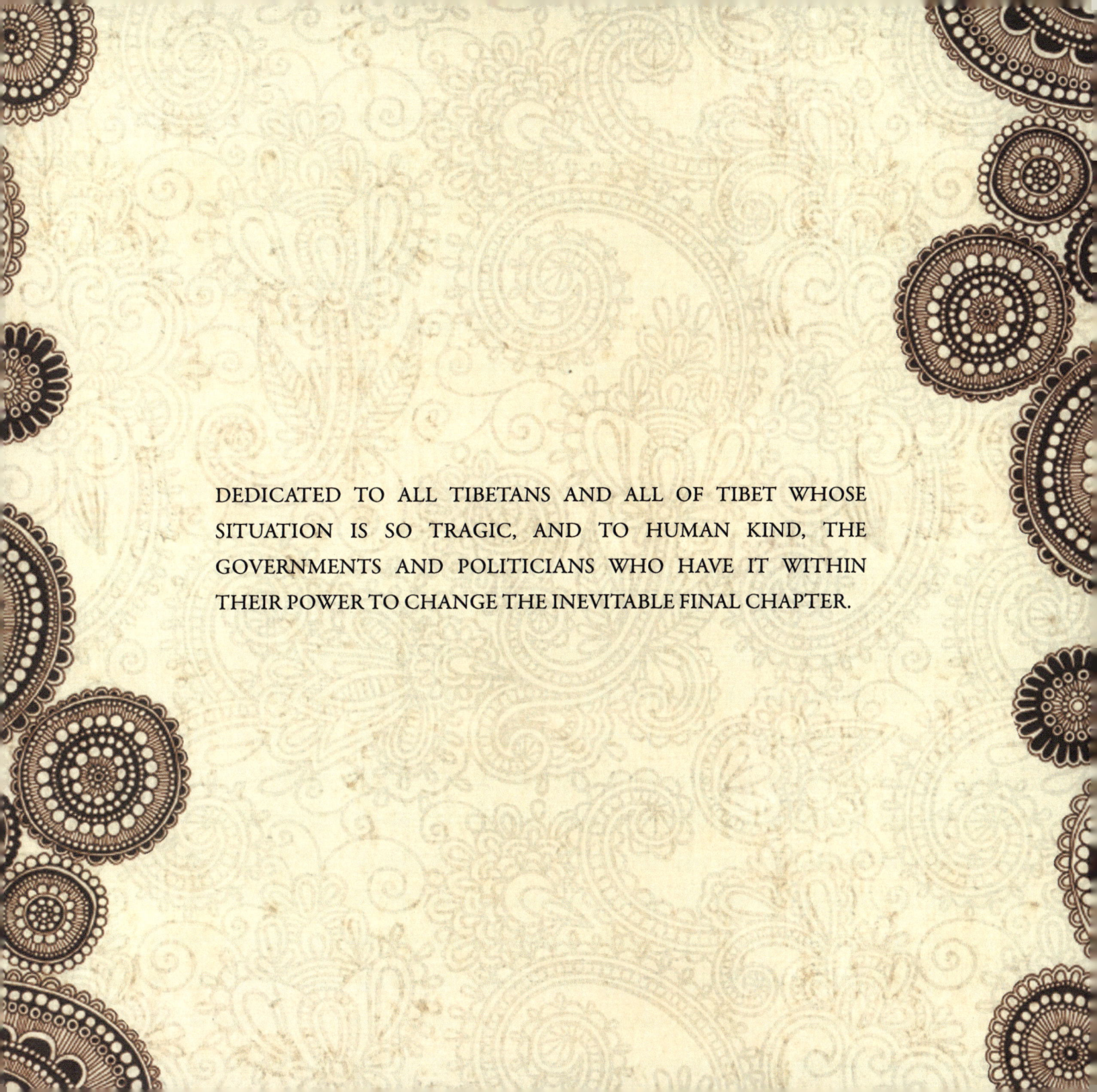

DEDICATED TO ALL TIBETANS AND ALL OF TIBET WHOSE SITUATION IS SO TRAGIC, AND TO HUMAN KIND, THE GOVERNMENTS AND POLITICIANS WHO HAVE IT WITHIN THEIR POWER TO CHANGE THE INEVITABLE FINAL CHAPTER.

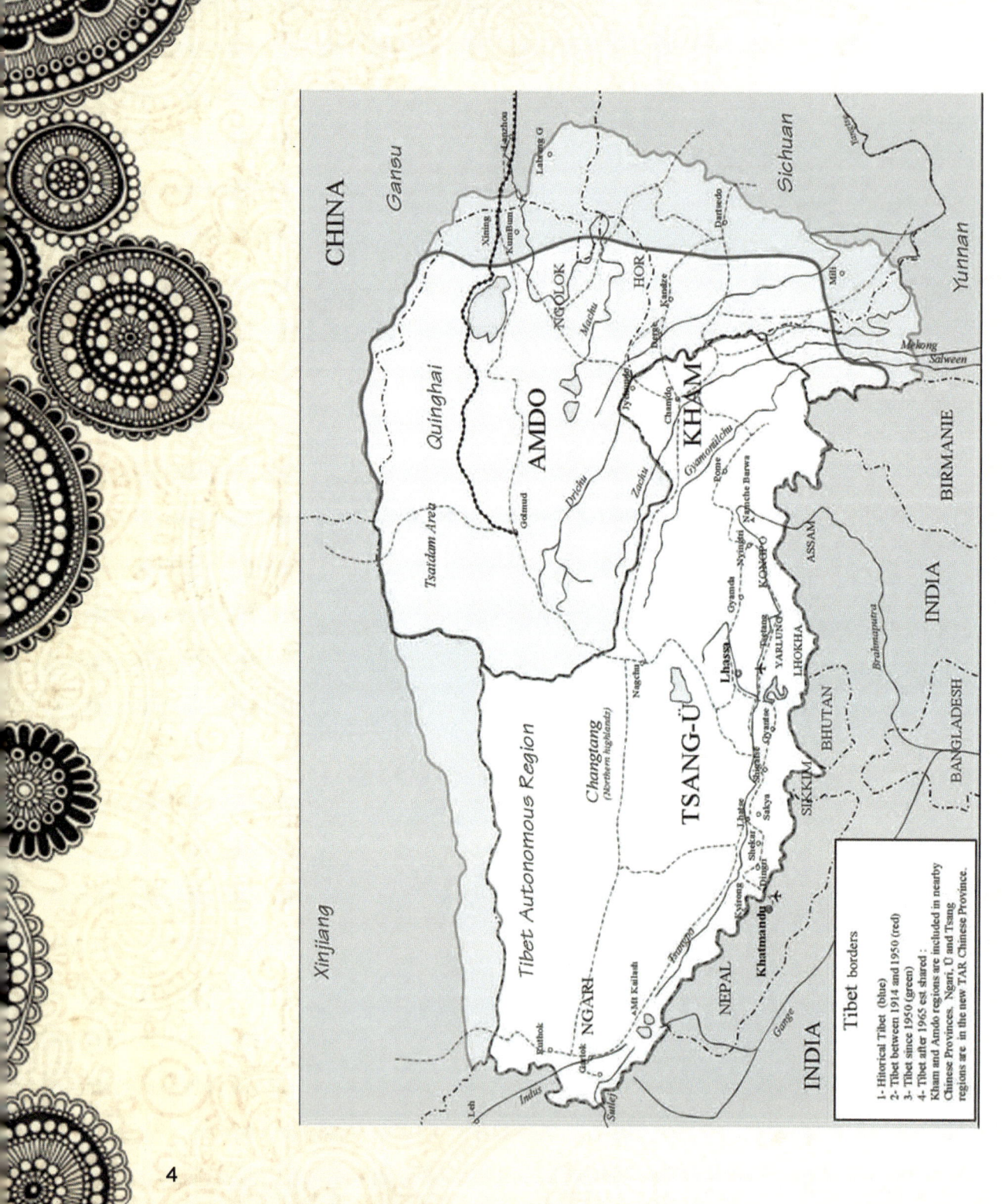

This is the journal of my trip to India, Nepal and Tibet between the 9th May and 21st June 2009 and to complete the Khora around the sacred mountain, Mt. Kailash during the month of Saga Dawa. I give all merit accumulated, to the lives of the Tibetans who remain amidst inconceivable suffering.

This is a true account of forty two days from one person's lifetime; magnified in a way that enables the reader to share in the dreams and destiny of the author. It combines profound moments with tears and laughter, just three of the elements necessary for making the most of life.

My thanks to Izzie, who took care of all the cats and made this possible

CHANGI AIRPORT. SINGAPORE SATURDAY MAY 9th

The kites that once adorned the vaulted ceilings of the old terminal are gone. Twenty three years ago when I came through here with a husband and two small boys, that was the most there was to entertain them—that and running up and down the long terminal building. Now the array of gadgets, gizmos, iPods and ePods leaves me feeling as though I have been irretrievably catapulted into the digital world, without escape. I am helpless in one of the Airport gadget shops and stare blankly, trying to pinpoint what I need for my newly acquired digital camera. The days of working with my good old Pentax SLR with rolls of film are long gone. Now it is all about memory cards, memory sticks and the like. The trouble is, one has to have a good memory of the sequence of button pushing to make these new cameras do as they are told! The shop assistant helps me, with a mixture of disbelief and sympathy, at my lack of knowledge and technical ability especially as all I require is a memory card with lots of bytes!

The calm of the small koi pond and orchid garden, now part of the modern terminal building, is quite relaxing after 20 hours on the move. I sit for a short time before realising that it is a magnet for those with the latest cameras who go home with those last memories of 'Joan and Me at the koi pond—Changi airport!'. Everything recorded dated, magnified and highlighted. A group of Americans sitting next to me are talking. Sure enough I hear: "now we can show them back home we have seen the flower and fish garden at Singapore airport". Opening the book that is to become my memory of the next forty two days, the virgin paper awaits my thoughts. The pen is to become my dancer, moving over blank pages, as a ballerina moves over her stage. The months of

rehearsal long forgotten. Darkness holds the audience, waiting for the story to unfold. The scenes are set, and her graceful movement takes them on a journey she hopes they will never forget.

Struggling with lack of sleep and with a further two hours to go before boarding for Delhi, I offer the coffee guy my last 4 Singapore dollars for a 6 dollar coffee. It is one in the morning—he doesn't argue.

INDIA

MAY 10TH–MAY 23 2009

INDIRA GANDHI AIRPORT. DELHI SUNDAY MAY 10th.

As I come out of Delhi airport into the early morning haze, all my senses come instantly to life—the sounds, the aromas filling the air, the bustle and that familiar taste that pervades all of Asia. My driver is here on cue, thank goodness. I don't recognize anything from those days in the early seventies, before the husband and the children. So much building finished and unfinished, miles of construction, extension to the new metro, football stadium, roads, apartments, hotels. Running alongside all this are the shanty homes, the shacks, people bathing under one tap, a game of cricket in amongst piles of rubbish and dust, packs of dogs and of course the Brahmin cows. Monkeys making a nuisance of themselves, as they do, scatter as clods of mud are hurled at them. This urban sprawl probably connects within itself but not with the affluent Delhi that keeps it in its shadow.

The Yatri guesthouse offers a quiet calm whilst I adjust to the fact that I am back in India after 35 years. Indian cinnamon tea is brought to the small cool courtyard where I write, cases still on the path, with no sign of my host. After 2 hours it is now 9.30am, he, Sanjay Puri, finally appears. It hadn't occurred to me that the long wait may have been down to a double booking—it is! "Please wait a little longer and we will have your room ready" I sign the very large guestbook, am given the Sunday papers—oh, the joy

of travelling in India in the midst of a general election! The papers are full of political wrangling and not much else. I note that the current Indian government is to increase security along its Northern border, well aware that China is pushing further down into Tibet. With Nepal now under Maoist control and in a state of political turmoil, the peace buffer that Tibet once provided has disappeared along with its culture, religion, people and the spiritual and temporal leader His Holiness the Dalai Lama.

The privacy and comfort of a room finally arrives. I am relieved to be out of the 40 degree heat and surprised at my ability to be patient for 3 hours! It's not the Ritz, but the shower and a noisy fan work as does a plasma TV almost the length of one wall! The houseboy takes great delight in showing me all its bells and whistles and nearly gets a round of applause! Totally exhausted I sleep for an hour or so before the change in time zone gets me up and ready for an explore. I have no Indian rupees but know that despite it being Sunday, the major hotels will have currency exchange. I head out on foot into the noon Delhi heat—first mistake! The pollution is choking, the noise deafening and the heat scorching. I realize my mistake half an hour into the walk so decide to head back. I must have looked rather overcome as a young man stopped and asked if I was ok. I am immediately on my guard and decline his offer of assistance. He persists and good sense prevails as I finally trust his repeated offer of help. He hails a tuktuk and 10 minutes later I am back at the Yatri. He pays the fare and hopes I have a pleasant stay in India. My trust in fellow human beings is restored, and the fact that I am old enough to be his mother was probably enough to quash any idea that he might kidnap me to the red light district!

MAY 11TH

I join a Swiss couple the next morning at breakfast. They are off trekking in the Northern region on their first visit to India. I have another day in Delhi before catching the 9.30pm Jammu mail train to Pathankot, which will arrive at 7am to be followed by a 5 hour bus ride to Dharamsala.

Equipped with water and Indian rupees obtained right across the road, I take a tuktuk to the north east of Connaught Circus, which is the centre of New Delhi, to Lodi Road. Here I find Tibet House and museum with the wonderful Lodi gardens opposite. The roller coaster, death defying ride takes me through the social economic parallel once again—beggars, families living under plastic sheeting and corrugated iron, vast quantities of rubbish and general filth. Ordinary low income or no income people coagulate into a hot steamy stinking mess, under the hoardings for Hugo Boss, Calvin Klein and the $600 per night hotels. Sanjay had assured me things were better than before, a more reliable phone system, the new metro and shopping malls, I wonder if the inhabitants of the miles of slums I had driven past would agree.

I enter Tibet House and the one and only room that constitutes the museum, testimony to what little is left. A beautiful display of Thankas, some damaged, hang around the walls. A small display case houses some old statues of Shakyamuni

Buddha and other deities dating back to the 16th and 17th centuries. There is a wonderful ornate Tibetan saddle and some musical instruments including a pair of exquisitely decorated conch shells used in many of the chants. My heart skips a beat when I come to a tiny display of Tibetan currency and postage stamps. It had never occurred to me about money and here it was. Just 3 notes 6 coins and 6 stamps, but so beautiful. I am drawn to them like a moth to a light. A small library adjoins. Beautifully wrapped bundles of Buddhist scripts line one wall, hundreds of books in both Sanskrit and Tibetan and English fill the remaining space. Two young Tibetans work studiously in silence cataloging piles of new books and translations. I realize I have been in this tiny building for 2 hours! A bookshop is my last stop before the exit, and to my disgust it is run by Indians. The only part of this place that makes money and it is not going to the Tibetans. The change in attitude is dramatic. The sales pitch, the intolerance that I might just like to look round. I leave quickly after purchasing a calendar.

I find the Lodi Gardens, opposite, unexpectedly large. There are some magnificent old buildings, a bird park, and a labyrinth of paths all leading to specialist areas with an inviting restaurant set amongst the stunning array of foliage and fauna. I am given a guided tour. There are four levels all built in bamboo and what looks like teak with waterfalls, quiet rest areas and a choice of fan cooled inside eating areas or balcony dining. I am beginning to feel a little apprehensive about asking for the menu as this place is obviously for that well heeled population, however once seated, I find the Vietnamese salad and grilled chicken followed by the house special of chocolate mint mousse hasn't broken the bank!

The first of my language difficulties happens on the way back to the Yatri guesthouse. "No, this isn't right." I try to make the driver of the noisy tuktuk hear. The beginning of an argument is brewing, but then I find the guesthouse business card and hope that he can read English better than he speaks it! After much protesting he agrees to rectify the mistake, "bloody English" I shout and we both laugh. With a couple of hours still to kill before I catch the taxi to Old Delhi station, and the fact that my cases are back on the path due to it being check out time and the room is obviously needed, I decide to try the metro that everyone has been praising. I need water and a few things for the long journey.

The procedure for going just one stop on the Metro is best described in numbered stages. 1) Buy a token, easy. 2) miss the security check and get hauled back. 3) Wait whilst they deliberate if I am to go through the male or female body search. 4) Recover from the embarrassment of stage 3. 5) Try and work out how the wretched token opens the barrier. Finally get help which adds to embarrassment. 6) Try to find the correct platform, take a guess and discover I am on the wrong side of the tracks. 7) retrace steps to correct side. 8) When auto doors open wonder how on earth I can fit in amongst the sea of humanity that is before me. 9) Travel the one stop without dissolving from the heat and squeeze out of the carriage before the doors close. 10) Try and work out which is the correct exit, have several attempts before I hit the right one. I am now in designer Delhi, glitz, glamour glitter and greed. I complete my humble purchases and head back down to the

metro. This time I only get as far as repeating stages 1 and 2 before there is a hitch! At the body search—NO LIGHTERS ALLOWED. Why this hadn't been spotted on the way here, maybe they were just too engrossed as to whether I was a man or a woman! Now this is the only lighter I have and two women security people want to confiscate it! They must be making a fortune selling confiscated lighters! I go into reverse, push back through the queue of disgruntled metro goers, give my token away and am back on the street looking for the good old tuktuk! The elderly driver, with good English, engages me in conversation with the intention that I wouldn't realize we are going round in circles. I finally protest then discover I have no small change, nor of course does he, so end up paying double fare!!. All in all to purchase two bottles of water at cost 30 rupees and to experience the Delhi metro nearly gets me arrested twice, my gender questioned, my one and only guaranteed to work lighter nearly confiscated, being taken for a ride, literally, by a devious old tuktuk driver with an overall cost 80 rupees! And this is only day 2!

At 7.30.pm the taxi arrives to take me to Old Delhi station. We seem to spend most of the 30 minute journey on 2 wheels and the horn on continuous full blast mode. The old part of Delhi is no place for tourists these days let alone a single woman at 8 o clock at night, and I can see why. My white face in the back of a taxi is already causing attention. I am unceremoniously dumped at the station entrance amidst hundreds and hundreds of Indians, not a white face to be seen. My bag weighs too much and I struggle through yet another security check. The display board is not much help being in Hindi, but I locate an information room where my limited knowledge of cricket seems to be a bargaining tool for train and platform information! Deal done, Shane Warne seems to have clinched it! It's a long walk over the footbridge but the sight of a number of rats both below on the tracks and scurrying up various stages of the bridge I am on is enough to keep me going at a brisk pace despite the weight of my bag. Half of India seems to be waiting for the Jammu mail train no. 4033 which is nowhere to be seen. I later discover half of India IS waiting for this train as an important Hindu festival is taking place in Jammu. The NO SMOKING sign seems ridiculous considering I am standing in a considerable amount of litter, dust, fumes and general pollution. Do as the rest of India does, park bags, sit on bags, and ignore sign!

The train pulls in and the predicted scramble begins. Passenger lists are posted on the sides of the carriages, so I start the search for carriage A1 seat 3. J. COMER. A2 and A3 are located; all the B's, the first class carriage H, then come to the economy section and the free for all. NO WAY, I would rather walk. I start trudging with a lead weight for a bag up and down the platform, carriage after carriage but no coach A1. In a panic I plead with anyone that can understand, to help. "Wait here" it's further down", no it's back the other way" is all I am told. I push onto the first class carriage, determined to be on the train at least, and immediately told to get off by what seems to be private security for some VIP. Finally I spot a white face, rush over and give this unsuspecting woman a big hug! "You do speak English don't you" A broad American accent puts me in the picture, carriage A1 has yet to be attached, I burst into tears. She is from Hawaii, and on her way to Dharamsala to study *Vispassana* meditation, the very thing I did in 1973. The carriage arrives hastily coupled to the rest of the train and we pile in. Now I search for berth 3. Most of the numbers are missing but by calculation and guesswork, I find I am on a lower

berth near the door. It is very cramped and the berths are replicas of the old prison bunk system, just a board supported by chains attached to the wall. A sheet and blanket comes flying in and the chap opposite proceeds, very methodically, to cover his board with the sheet, complete with hospital corners! I stifle my laughter.

Finally we are off albeit very slowly! I notice a sign above the very dirty window. It reads: 'Pest and rat control inspection was completed in March'—comforting or not! The hasty coupling of the carriage has left an unusually large gap; I watch the tracks flash past underneath, finally fall asleep.

I wake just before sunrise and find the main door wide open, well this is India! Hanging onto the handrail I watch India go past at rather a leisurely speed. This is a mail train, not an express, so we stop at every little settlement. I see that no one is travelling on the roof as was customary in the 70's. I believe this practice is now banned. A well spoken, very tall middle age man joins me at the door and starts talking about his years in Canada. The mention of Canada brings pangs of guilt over the fact that I have not told either of my two sons that I am here, Matthew lives in Canada. Anyhow this chap lived there for ten years before his family arranged a marriage to a doctor, whom he had never met or even seen except in a photo. She works for the Government Health Department, earning a good salary, and he was obliged to give Canada up and return to Delhi. He is very knowledgeable about the different styles of housing that we are passing. I am fascinated by the beautiful, ornate homes that stand four stories high. These are the homes of the Punjabi Sikhs who control the lucrative farming region through which we are passing.

The train stops at a large station where there is the frantic rush to get off, find the tea wallah, purchase tea and get back before the train leaves. So under the guidance of my friend who stays on the train and bellows instructions I rush along the platform, barge to the front of the queue—women are permitted to do this—and with plastic cup burning my fingers, follow the sound of my friends guiding shouts, trying to dodge the throng and keep the tea in the cup. Well, half of it has stayed there and I savour every sip! I keep my place at the open carriage door for the remainder of the journey and suddenly we are here, at Pathankot. I scramble to retrieve my bag, farewell the chap with the hospital corners, who during passing conversation about why I was here and where I was going next, had become convinced I am a spy for the Tibetan Government-in-exile! I find my American friend and we set off through the throng to find the bus station and the local bus to Dharamsala.

TUESDAY MAY 12TH

Absolute chaos, Pathankot hasn't changed; there is just more of it. Lorries, cars, motorbikes, horse drawn carts, dogs, cows, people, all going in different directions through the dust and the early morning heat. It is 7am. We find the bus station and receive the customary instructions: "You wait here, bus goes in 1 hour" I stand patiently next to a pile of old oil drums and a mangy dog. This hardly looks like the bus stop to me! Without any warning and well before schedule the bus is here and being loaded up. There is the usual scramble

for a seat. This is the last leg of a very long journey, 4 days on the move, these last 5 hours travelling cost NZ$3! I settle into a window seat and a battle begins with the occupant of the seat in front who obviously wants his bit of the window open and slides the glass back to shut my part. I push the glass back and ram my elbow into the window frame. A game of arm wrestling begins, I protest when he gives it such a shove I nearly lose my arm altogether! The bus has very little suspension and the road surface is rough to say the least. By the time we get to our first tea stop my spine feels as though it has concertinaed into the base of my neck. The American buys all sorts of edibles to which I give a miss then it's back to the arm wrestling!

At 11am we finally arrive in Dharamsala. Most of the locals disembark and are replaced with a motley assortment of foreigners reminiscent of bygone hippy era for the last leg of this journey to McCleod Ganj. I have been on the move for 15 hours and experienced the delights of both the Indian rail network and the local bus service. The new passengers seem to be mostly American and French, the dreadlocks, bells, bangles and mala beads all in great abundance. The green beedies, which are a dried leaf, rolled up tight and held together with a red thread and then smoked, are still around and I hear bits of low tone conversation about hanging out here or perhaps there. It is all rather like a time warp except I am in the mother/ granny group now! The last 5kms are incredibly steep and narrow and the bus teeters precariously close to the edge. I don't look. There it is, the town of McCleod Ganj, built into a hillside, the home of the Tibetan Government-in-exile and the Dalai Lama the spiritual and temporal leader of the Tibetan people.

McCLEOD GANJ. The American and I share the cost of hiring a porter, with incredibly long legs and a very large turban, to carry the bags up a steep hill to the Pema Thang guesthouse. Hundreds of prayer flags stretch down from the roof across my balcony and join the surrounding trees. My room is modest but adequate with a working shower, a small kitchen, and a breathtaking view of the Kangra Valley. I look in the mirror as I run a welcome shower and realize I am black from head to foot from standing in the open doorway on the train. It brings back memories of travelling on the roof of a train in the seventies, and then it took days of scrubbing to get clean! After restoring myself to nearly my normal colour, I find the guesthouse restaurant and order a large bowl of fruit salad and four cappuccinos. Better not to sleep now, so off to explore and see how much has changed since 1974. It has, dramatically. Dozens of stalls line the now partially sealed but still narrow roads. Cars, motorbikes, taxis push their way through the mass of tourists, mostly of the same ilk that I had traveled on the bus with. Tourist Tibet is everywhere, as are the banners FREE TIBET, FREE THE PANCHEN LAMA, and the Tibetan flag flies high over most rooftops. It feels wonderful, but tinged with a little sadness that after all these years the Tibetans have been pushed to the fringes, to make way for the large number of guesthouses and hotels needed to accommodate the global followers of their spiritual leader. I suppose it makes economic sense but I soon see that most of the more lucrative sights, shops and hotels are owned by Indians, cashing in on the Tibetan Cause at this Buddhist Mecca. I wander for a while soaking up the atmosphere. There are huge smiles from every Tibetan accompanied by the words 'tashi deleh', the Tibetan greeting, or hands clasped together and a slight bow of the head, I am so at home here already.

WEDNESDAY MAY 13ᵀᴴ

I am up to watch the beautiful sunrise at 5am. The prayer flags catch the newborn rays of light and then release them with every breath of the breeze, it is captivating. I meet the American for breakfast and she suggests we go to Sidhbari, the home of the Karmapa, head of the Kagyu lineage, the lineage that I study with back in New Zealand. Sonam, Pema Thang's manager, tells us that Wednesday is the day for public audience with the rather elusive young man who, it is rumoured, may succeed the Dalai Lama if the Tibetan Buddhist tradition of reincarnation is broken. as the Chinese have recently declared that one has to have a permit to be reborn—absurd. The young Karmapa may have the responsibility of the future of Tibet and its people.

The Norbulingka Institute is on the same route so we decide to visit there first. As we walk the 15 minutes to the local bus stand the American ducks into nearly every shop we pass and I soon discover she is quite a shopaholic. Needless to say she is loaded up with purchases before we start our journey! The local bus is packed full of hot and sweaty locals. We pass through Dharamsala and then onto quite a good road that takes us through village after village. This bus route is obviously geared up to locations of need rather than an inflexible predetermined route, not once is there an empty seat or place to stand. The journey takes 30 minutes and we find ourselves standing on the side of a dusty road with a steep walk of 20 minutes ahead to Norbulingka. A group of monks in a share taxi manage to squeeze us in, thank goodness, and eventually arrive to find just about everyone is at lunch! Having miscalculated the time needed to get here and my friend's frequent shop stops we only have 30 minutes before we need to continue onto Sidhbari, little time to glimpse the beauty of this place. I will come back—unaccompanied! The American heads straight for the Institute shop. I wonder how she will cope being confined to one building when she starts her *vispassana* course and where long periods of silence and fasting are adhered to. I follow; discover this shop is wonderful—and wonderfully expensive! Hand knotted Tibetan carpets, altar tables, beautifully carved boxes, ornate tables and cabinets, and a breathtaking display of appliqué thankas are all on sale. I watch with amusement as my American friend whirls round, choosing this and then finding something better. Item after item is chosen and then discarded for another and all the while continuous exclamations of delight at the work that has been put into everything that is here. Finally she selects a beautiful brocade and appliqué wall hanging of the eight auspicious symbols of Buddhism. I smile—the same symbols as the tattoo adorning my back! Next comes the paperwork and the credit card—she is shipping this straight back to America—well Hawaii. I wait patiently and seriously doubt that she will get through her 10 day course where "I want" has never been heard of.

The 15 minute walk downhill back to the road is easy despite still being loaded up with all the shopping from McCleod Ganj. We catch another bus and travel another 10 minutes before arriving at Sidhbari. The huge ornate residence of the Karmapa is set against a backdrop of the Himalayas and with a perfect sky of azure blue the whole

picture is breathtaking. The golden wheel of Dharma flanked by the 2 deer, representing the deer park at Sarnath where Buddha gave his first teaching, sits high on the entrance and is ablaze with the rays of the afternoon sun. A huge crowd is already here, queuing to get through security. After a very long wait we finally make it inside the huge hall, I can not estimate the number here. Suddenly everyone is on their feet as the Karmapa makes his entrance, I lose track of what is happening as his audience again starts to form queues down the aisles. Every person holds *Khatas*, the white silk scarf that is the traditional gift representing peace. I present mine; it is touched to the head of the Karmapa and returned, again tradition, with a single strand of red thread. He does not speak, and sadly the audience is over. I feel somewhat disappointed that after all the waiting he didn't utter a word. I learn later that this is what often happens—so different from the Dalai Lama, with his famous laugh, big smile and time for everyone. Once outside I chat with some monks in the hope that they might know Lama Pasang, the resident Lama back in New Zealand. I leave a message at the secretary's office conveying Lama's greetings on his behalf. Most of the buildings in the complex are closed to the public.

It is now time to find the means to get back to McCleod Ganj. We share a jeep all the way, which is slightly more comfortable than the bus. Again the suspension is put to the test by the road surface which is barely distinguishable from the rest of the hillside. I am rather hoping the American decides to do things on her own tomorrow as she is now at the forever complaining stage!

The staff at the Pema Thang are easy going, always have a smile and are keen to chat. The food is mostly simple Tibetan, *momos*—steamed dumplings filled with either meat or vegetables; *thukpa*—which is the same sort of thing only in a broth and extremely filling.; *tenthook*—glass noodles again in a broth plus a few western variations on the same theme. It is all incredibly cheap NZ$10 a day is more than adequate for breakfast and dinner. With a little extra for my self indulgent moment most afternoons, a cappuccino at the Moonpeak cafe!

THURSDAY MAY 14TH AND FRIDAY MAY 15TH

The American has gone to start her course. My day starts with those sunrises, each one different but evoking the same feelings of peace and contentment. Their magic bathes the valley below and traverses the Himalayas that surround, all the while the sound of the prayer flags sing their mantras. I hold these moments close as I go down the hill to the main temple to complete a *kora*, a clockwise walk around the temple perimeter. The prayer wheels are constantly spinning with numbers of people paying their respects to *Shakyamuni*, the present Buddha; *Chenrezig*, the embodiment of compassion; *Manjushri*, embodiment of wisdom. A few have already started their prostrations, mostly Tibetan but I see the occasional westerner. I have made friends with a visiting monk from Ladakh, in the northern most part of India where the Tibetan refugees are to be found in considerable numbers, and we sit for a while sometimes engaged in conversation, sometimes in silence. That is the best time as the difficulty with the language does not interfere with what is being silently spoken.

Back for breakfast, apple pancakes definitely my favorite with a pot of coffee, then a wander round the stalls and small shops hunting for the gifts I intend taking back, not only for the boys and close friends, but as many as possible for some of those people that have made this journey possible for me. I have quite a lot of fun with this, coffee cups with Buddhist symbols for Neil and Jan, as they sell coffee from Vanuatu. Thick woollen gloves for Eileen as she is out in all weathers with the sheep, and so on.

On Thursday afternoon I head out to the children's village where Tenzin, the boy I have sponsored for 4 years, arrived from Tibet. Sadly for me he has moved onto a college miles away in Mussoorie and I haven't the time for that journey. I am greeted at the gate by a small boy asking for money, the first Tibetan I have come across begging. I ask him a few directions, and then suggest if he returns to his class, where I am sure he should be, and draw me a nice picture, I would consider buying it. He ponders this, thinks it is not a bad idea, so we both walk up to the school, he to his classroom and I to find the reception. There are children everywhere, all in uniform, all smiling, laughing, and so polite. I find the office and they do not hesitate to find me a guide for a short tour of the school. She is a young woman, in her early twenties, who came across the Himalayas as a child, accompanied by her father who then returned. This is quite common for a parent to cross the mountains with a child, bringing it to safety and, to avoid being repatriated as the Chinese call it, then return themselves. Sadly so many of them are arrested on their return and imprisoned for many years. Some never make it out. My friend now works for the school in the office. We chatted about the curriculum, which includes all the basics, Tibetan, English and Hindi language and Buddhist philosophy. The dormitories are spotless and bright, every under five has a teddy bear on his or hers bed. About 2000 children reside here, all reliant on sponsors, donations of money, clothes, toys and school equipment. It is an enormous task for the small organization first started by the Dalai Lama's sister Jetsun Pema. The commitment and behaviour of the children I met would leave many schools in New Zealand and England wanting!

We touched on the recent move by the Chinese to grab these children back to the motherland. Any parent with a child here and who is employed by Chinese in any job, or is reliant on a pension or any other Government money, will have everything taken away if they do not bring their child back. I am told quite a lot have returned, the parents being so afraid of the consequences. Once back however, it is believed the child is confiscated by the authorities and taken, usually hundreds of miles, to a re-education centre. Here they are indoctrinated with all things Chinese. Everything Tibetan is banned—the language, clothes, religion, all including the Dalai Lama is condemned, ridiculed and liable for severe punishment if not adhered to. These are the lost children of Tibet. This conversation has brought us both to tears and we hug, praying for it to stop.

I have some fun in the kindergarten finding two, of the fifty mentally and physically handicapped, both with downs syndrome, just wonderful. Both are boys aged 3 and 4 and it is memorable experience to be with them—both are real charmers. Their parents' location and status—unknown; the status of the boys—refugee.

The office promises to contact Tenzin. I know he will be as upset as I am not to have met—next time perhaps. With the many hugs and farewells ringing in my ears I exit the

school gates feeling that my miniscule amount of support is pitiful and determined that once back in New Zealand I can do a lot more. Across the road from the school is the Dal lake, listed in the guide books as a place to visit. It turns out to be a filthy brackish pond frequented by the locals—evident with the amount of rubbish, discarded remnants of lunch and other unmentionable amounts of human waste. There are few people here—not surprising—and it certainly does not warrant "a place to see" listing!

FRIDAY MAY 15TH

After my usual morning, I walk the long, steep, uphill, two kilometer walk to TIPA, the Tibetan Institute of Performing Arts. I had seen their performance at the Bruce Mason centre in Takapuna, New Zealand, two years ago, and had enjoyed every minute. All this hill walking is standing me in good stead for what lies ahead when I finally reach Tibet. The views are breathtaking. McCleod Ganj looks like a living balancing act precariously entwined into the hillside. For the Tibetans, life here IS a fragile balancing act precariously entwined with the Indian Goverment. TIPA turns out to be a bit of a disappointment. A group of students in national dress, chatter, huddled in a corner of the courtyard; they do not make any effort to acknowledge me. With nothing much to see I do not stay long.

SATURDAY MAY 16TH

I decide to phone Janet. I have been trying hard not to think too much about the boys, the cats and the cattery but give into it today! It is reassuring to hear the familiar voice telling me things are fine at home. All the cats ok including Blossom and Lucy both of whom have difficult health issues. Izzie is evidently coping well. Numbers are down but June bookings are looking better. Daniel, one of my sons, phoned the day after I left and being totally in the dark as to where I am, thought Izzie had said I was at the vet and asked how long I would be. Obviously he was quite confused when her reply "about 6 weeks" was the answer, and even more confused when she followed on "no, not the vet, your Mum is in Tibet". The little phone booth I am in is shaking as I fall about laughing.

Deciding to take the rest of the day easy as I seem to have done such a lot in what is only the first week, I go back to Pema Thang for some quiet reading. I am the only person on the restaurant balcony and immersed in a recently purchased copy of *Drinking The Mountain Stream*, songs and poems of Milarepa, Tibet's beloved saint, who was also responsible for most of Tibetan opera—yes there is such a thing!

"Can I join you" comes the Dutch accent. A tall woman in check shirt, jeans and leather cowboy boots sits down. In this heat her apparel looks a little ridiculous! She introduces herself, Jacqui, and starts chatting. She is working here for a week helping the radio station—*Voice of Tibet*—to improve its service. Apparently, they are able to get a 15 minute fragmented broadcast into Lhasa most days, but it seems they have run into problems. Jacqui is a foreign correspondent, focusing on human rights issues, has her

own radio programme in Holland, and she tells me of some of the many hotspots she has been in—Palestine, Israel, Africa and here to the Tibetan community many times. She is married to an Irishman, so the many years of conflict there with the IRA is an issue for which she has a deep understanding. After listening for some time, I realize this is a serious woman, not the run of the mill tourist. It turns out that the manager, Sonam, with whom I have spoken in some depth about my forthcoming trip into Tibet, has pointed me out to her. We move on to the subject of my trip and the need for people who are going to Tibet to help the community here with any reports of the current situation. Sonam has already furnished me with a book, published by the Tibetan Government-in-Exile, of information they find useful. Since the major crackdown, one of many, by the Chinese in response to the 10 March protests communication with Lhasa has all but ceased. Hundreds were killed in March and an estimated 5000 more have been arrested and disappeared. My Dutch friend organizes for me to meet two reporters for lunch on Monday at the main Government building. Suddenly things are taking on a much more serious feel.

I need some fresh air after this unexpected change in direction and to consider how far I can get involved. I am due to team up with nine other people, as the Chinese will not allow solo travellers, so nothing I do can affect them. Walking through the narrow streets reflecting on the last couple of hours, I stop at rather a "posh shop", the window of which contains some beautiful statues. I glance up at the name above the door, Ancient Treasures of Tibet. It is a large shop compared to most, selling a wide array of items from CDs and incense to *thankas* and carpets. At the far end is a beautiful display of statues, *Shakyamuni*, The *Taras*, *Chenrezig* etc, all of different sizes and quality. I spot a magnificent image of *Manjushri*, one of the best I have seen. A polite young Tibetan offers me a seat and a cup of tea and brings the figure to the table. It is beautiful. I listen to its history, which may or may not be accurate, and am then told the price! Sadly it has to go back to the cabinet, although I am sorely tempted. The young man brings out several images of *Shakyamuni*, some obviously modern and machine tooled with the painted face. I study each one for some time and finally decide on one of the smallest in the group, but a design I have not seen anywhere else and which is quite different from the rest on the table. This is the special purchase I have been promising myself for years, one which I had planned to buy in Tibet, but with the situation unknown there I am not sure what is available to buy and also how much is made by the Chinese. So *Shakyamuni*, the present Buddha, is to be purchased here. It is carefully packed in bubble-wrap with a cloth outer wrapping and I continue what is developing into my shopping day with the purchase of Tibetan brocade blouses for my daughter-in-law Anna and Lucy who is shortly to become my second daughter-in-law. I buy a beautiful Tibetan silver bracelet, each link engraved, for my son Daniel, and a bagful of different things for friends back in New Zealand.

Back at the Pema Thang I find Jaqui and we have dinner together. The conversation is a little less serious and I learn a little about my new friend's life as a Foreign correspondent and her family. I think she is a little bemused when she discovers that this pro-Tibetan activist and devotee of the Dalai Lama, actually runs a hotel for cats back in New Zealand!

Suddenly the weather takes a turn for the worse—the first rain I have experienced since arriving in India. The power goes off, and I fumble my way back to my room with the aid of a lighter. There are candles on hand. A real storm is brewing. The wind is up and I can hear thunder still some way off. I open the doors to the balcony. The prayer flags are screaming, their lines taught as the first flash of lightning strikes. The entire valley is momentarily lit up, the pines are almost horizontal but still manage to support the lines that hold he hundreds of prayer flags. Another great bang of thunder resonates across the valley accompanied by the second flash of lightning, this one almost overhead. Strangely, the rain has stopped but the wind is deafening. The heavens are in battle. The great hammer of thunder versus the steel blade of lightning with the roar of the wind filling the valley, turning unexpectedly one way then another. A giant amphitheatre of sound and light and with one spectator—me! I have no idea how long this continues, but am aware when the final crescendo hits McCleod Ganj. The thunder retreats. The wind abates and all is relatively quiet. Everything looks exhausted. The flags and trees seem to sigh with relief. I, too, am quite exhausted and feel privileged to have experienced such a contest here, high up in the Himalayas.

SUNDAY MAY 17TH

After the storm last night it is a beautiful day, about 34°C nowhere near as hot and uncomfortable as Delhi. I ask Sonam about taking the Buddha I have purchased to the temple to be blessed; apparently this is possible. On the way to the temple I buy a handful of coloured, platted, wrist cords that are worn for good fortune. I understand the Tibetans in Tibet recognise these as being a sign from His Holiness the Dalai Lama that they are not forgotten, and make good gifts without arousing too much suspicion as they can be given discreetly. The central gathering place at the Temple seems to be busier than usual. I try to find some help with finding the right person to talk to about my request. I am sent to the butter lamp room where I am told an English speaking person is working, what a lovely way to spend the day, making butter lamps. I enter the small building, hundreds of lamps are aglow, and in amongst the twinkling lights I see a small, blonde woman, totally absorbed in her job. "Can I help" she looks up. The accent, I think, is Israeli, and on hearing what I am looking for, points me in the direction of a long building the other side of the main gathering centre, assuring me the Dalai Lama would bestow his blessings on my object. I had no idea the Dalai Lama was here, with heart pounding, I head to the security building she has pointed out. I am greeted by men in suits and leave the Buddha amongst all the x-ray machines, body scanners and other assorted security paraphenalia. I am told to return tomorrow after 9 am.

Trying to find a little peace and quiet here is proving more difficult than I expected. Other solo women travellers seek the security of sharing a table or suggesting joint ventures to here and there. I retreat to my room back at the Pema Thang. I can't help feeling that Tibetan culture, to all intent and purpose, is thriving here, but it has become somewhat abused by Western tourists. Indeed, the coloured thread bracelets I have bought to take to Tibet are, according to Sonam, things the Westerners have invented. Groups frequent the coffee shops and compare notes on their *Tushita* course or meditation classes, or the next

teaching they will attend. Mobile phones are in abundance as are laptops and internet cafes. It is all so packaged, all the boxes ticked off as they race through the lists of what to read, who to listen to, centres to attend etc, all a short cut to Nirvana. I have studied, albeit not as intensely as I would have liked, for 30 odd years and only scratched the surface of this immensely complex philosophy, the true experiential knowledge of *karma*, *bardo*, {the period between death and rebirth} and the various methods of meditation come with the joining of minds where no words are uttered, where the understanding and connection between teacher and student is, beyond all, the need for the conventional human perspectives. Most of the people I have met or quietly listened to, so far, never stop talking. Perhaps I am the one who has got it wrong!

I meet up with Jacqui and two of the reporters from Voice of Tibet at the Moonpeak cafe for coffee. This is proving to be a valuable introduction to some of the people I am to have lunch with tomorrow. I listen to the story of one of them, a young woman in her mid twenties named Decky, who was educated in China under her mothers authority. Evidently her parents had split when her mother went to work for the Chinese and her father refused to do the same—obviously determined not to relinquish his identity or beliefs. Decky had secured a place at University in Beijing but at the last minute had succumbed to her fathers continual pleas to return to Tibet and reaffirm that she was Tibetan, not Chinese. He then organized her exodus to Nepal crossing the Himalayas on foot, as thousands do, to escape the Chinese brutality and destruction of Tibet, and finally to India where she had finished her education and has ended up working here in McCleod Ganj for the radio station. Her father went back across the mountains only to be arrested by the Chinese, and died in prison—a story that so many tell. I can see the tears rolling down this young woman's cheek as she shows us a photo of her Dad. The sombre moment is broken by the sound of monks chanting, I see a large gathering of people coming down the hill all carrying a candle, all silent. Banners, FREE THE PANCHEN LAMA are carried by many, along with the Tibetan flag and FREE TIBET. This is the protest march I had seen the posters for, demanding once again, the release of the Panchen Lama, the world's youngest political prisoner, taken by the Chinese authorities 10 years ago. Despite worldwide condemnation of their action, they have never given any information as to what they have done with him. Worse still, they have appointed their own Panchen Lama whose place is in Beijing alongside the top echelons of the Chinese government. The Panchen Lama, is traditionally, the person who will search and recognize the next Dalai Lama, when the time comes, so this manoeuvre by the Chinese has, in their eyes, sorted that problem out ahead of time. I leave my companions and join the procession up to the Temple where prayers are being chanted. There is quite a gathering. Hundreds of candles twinkle in the twilight, casting faint but sufficient light on the faces of many of the gathering for me to see their real sorrow.

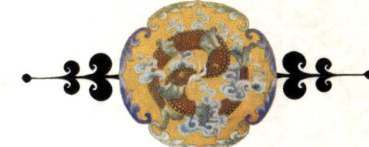

MONDAY MAY 18TH

I collect my precious items from security at 9 am. I have spent all last night wondering if it was possible to be granted a few moments with the Dalai Lama, an idea I have finally given up as it would be like knocking on the White House door and expecting to see Barack

Obama! It is another glorious day so decide to walk the two kilometres downhill to the Government offices for my meeting with The Voice of Tibet presenters. I am amazed to see a recently opened vet clinic, things are progressing. This is the quieter part of McLeod Ganj and I see various houses and rooms for rent and make a mental note for my next visit. The Government buildings are a maze of different rooms for each department. It takes me a while to find the room I am looking for, but I hear Jacqui's Dutch accent coming from an open door. A bank of computers line one wall of a comparatively small room with desks piled high with paperwork filling the remaining space. Not much room for visitors. The six people, all in headphones and totally engrossed in their tasks, are oblivious to my presence. I watch and can feel the highly charged atmosphere. Jacqui is in a small booth at the end of the room. Despite the glass door being closed I can still hear that she is speaking in Dutch and is obviously on air. She spots me and waves. Shifting some of the piles of papers, carefully, I make a space to sit and focus on trying to make some sense of what all these people are doing. Peering over the shoulder of the chap nearest, I watch the screen for several minutes, but I am none the wiser.

"Hi, you found us OK then. Let me introduce you" There are warm greetings from everyone and some attempt to explain what they are working on. Sadly computers and radio broadcasting is just not something I can easily absorb. My understanding of a mouse is a little furry thing that makes a lot of women scream! I feel quite relieved when Jacqui suggests we go for lunch.

The dining hall, which caters for all department workers, is almost full. There are people from many countries, but mostly Tibetans, the women in traditional dress, the men in western clothes. The two tables, very long, run through the middle of the hall, each table with a matching wooden bench. I follow Jacqui, grab a large tin plate and cutlery, and work my way round the cauldrons of rice, dhal, noodles, vegetables and meat, all very simple. We find a space but it is impossible to talk with the clatter of hundreds of tin plates. I think about the recent news report about the British government politicians running up huge expenses for their meals and the public outcry there has been now it is exposed. Perhaps the Brits ought to come and see how the Tibetans do things!

Once finished I take my plate to the exit, scrape off all unwanted into a large tin bath, put the plate and utensils into another tin bath full of water and follow the group back to the office. A middle age Tibetan in a suit greets us and invites me into a private office. This is the editor, the number one man, whose name is Karma. He is very well spoken and we go through the things that they would find helpful. Aside from general observing of military barracks, evidence of Tibetan children in school, Tibetans with a job etc, Karma also asks if I will take a number of matchboxes that have the new radio frequency printed inside and leave them in places I deem safe. The current frequency of the 'Voice of Tibet' has been detected by the Chinese and naturally blocked. This is the only contact those in Tibet have with the refugee community here. The new frequency probably won't last long but even a week is invaluable. I don't hesitate to accept all Karma's requests and make one suggestion of my own, that I take a handful of the small stickers that also have the radio details, and leave them in things, under things, or wherever they might be found by those who so desperately need a lifeline to the outside world. The meeting is now over, Jacqui returns to the broadcasting booth and I embark on the two kilometres return walk, uphill!

Finally the Pema Thang comes into view and I almost crawl the last 50 meters. I stumble into my room and collapse on the bed exhausted. I watch the sunset, horizontally, until the need for coffee overwhelms me. I find a new English couple in the restaurant and at first sight—oh what a sight! They are probably between 25 and 35 both with a mountain of dreadlocks piled high amongst old ribbon and beads, neck adornments of every description, tattoos visible through the tears and holes in their clothing and a toddler, in just a tee shirt, running amok. A French family, neat as a new pin, sits opposite, the comparison brings me to quiet laughter, this is life! I pick up the north of England accent. I try to immerse myself in my new book—impossible, as I end up with the toddler crawling under my table. "Sorry, he is being a handful" came that broad northern accent. "It's OK" is my short response. Having heard my English accent I am immediately engaged in conversation. It turns out they are from the Yorkshire Dales, here in India for the first time. He is a computer engineer and she is some type of therapist, although I can't ascertain exactly what in! They have decided to donate their month's holiday to working as volunteers, he at the Government offices helping upgrade their system and she at the one and only pre-school nursery. I have to admire them for their determination to help rather than ponder. Their boy, Luca, is 3 and yes he is a handful, but he too is taking India in his stride.

TUESDAY MAY 19TH

My time here is fast nearing its end, only 2 days before I go back to Delhi, then on to Nepal. I go into town to book my train seat back and am assured there will not be a problem. After three different travel offices I discover all trains are full, unless I want to pay the extortionate tourist rate. The alternative is a 13 hour bus ride. I book a seat on the 6.30pm departing Thursday scheduled to arrive 7.30am Friday at cost approx NZ$15. I don't expect too much for my money even though I am assured this is a deluxe coach!

I seek out a pharmacy on the way back to the guesthouse. I have discovered their dog has a number of ticks in his ears—hydrogen peroxide should do the trick. I find the dog, then find a rather brusque German lady, in her late fifties I guess, who is not best pleased at being interrupted from her book, but who looks the sort that will have everything. "Do you have any tweezers" I enquire. Thinking they are for my use she gladly disappears, returns with new tweezers, then watches horrified as I dose the dogs ears in fluid, wait a few moments, then proceed to grapple with reluctant ticks. Within a few moments, I have the hotel staff as an audience, intrigued at the job in hand and incredulous that the dog, a long hair Alsatian cross, is allowing such a thing. I learn later that this is not a dog to be messed with as a rule. Job done! A round of applause from my audience, a quick wipe of the tweezers, and I return them to their owner, who is still aghast over what use they had been put to. Almost in a state of feint she declines their return and departs the scene clutching her book with such force the whites of her knuckles are very visible! I wonder what course she is booked on, obviously one that is geared to harnessing rage and emotional ties to innate objects! I hope. Sonam seems quite

overwhelmed that I would spend money on the dog. As I hand him the bottle of fluid to keep for the next time as they will surely rein fest. "You may as well have the tweezers, donated by the nice German lady".

I head down to the temple. My friend from Ladakh is leaving this evening and I have promised to see him before he goes. I buy cookies and water on the way and chat to many of the stall holders that I seem to know so well already. Most sell much the same sort of thing—mala beads, turquoise bracelets or necklaces and assorted other jewelry. One or two have 'authentic old pieces', old leather bags, statues of the many deities and so on. The trouble is, the same genuine ancient one off items can be seen on more than one stall! The family selling padlocks is one of my favorites. Large, heavy and very ornate pieces with the most amazing lock system that sometimes works during a demonstration. If it fails it is taken home at the end of each day and returned in "good working order" for the next demonstration. I don't buy one but we have a laugh about the lock's apparent willfulness.

I find my friend sitting in the usual place, he has a huge smile. We chat a little about his return home when, suddenly, the peace is disturbed by a large male macaque (temple monkey) running along the balcony railings, chasing a couple of smaller ones. His pursuit falters as he spots my carrier bag, which does not seem any different to anyone else's. In a flash he bounds to the end of our bench and makes a grab for the bag. The monk and I are on our feet, my friend in retreat and me, well the bag aside from the cookies also has my camera, I lift the end of the heavy bench and start pushing it into the monkey. His investigation into the contents of his booty is momentarily lost as the bench gives him a thump in the stomach. Next thing the monk is back grabs me by the collar and pulls me back as the irritable ape starts to charge, dropping the bag and spilling out the contents. By now the entire floor of this part of the temple has been cleared and those that remain watch in horror as this crazy English lady tries to take on a large male macaque. The charge is only a threat, the contents of the bag are not forgotten, and he returns to examine the items strewn on the floor. He soon takes off with the cookies, leaving the water and my camera—thankfully he is not a budding photographer! Everyone breathes a sigh of relief and I realize my heart is pounding and I am dripping in sweat. I get a warning from my friend about tackling the temple monkeys, not that I have any intention of repeating the last ten minutes. I bid farewell to my friend; maybe one day we will meet again—then he is gone. My heart is touched with sadness as I wonder what the future has for him and the tens of thousands like him that remain displaced as refugees.

I find a quieter place to sit for a while, opposite the first of the large copper prayer wheels that encircle the inner part of the temple housing the giant *Shakyumuni* Buddha, the beautiful thousand armed *Avalokiteshvara* also known as *Chenrezig*, Guru Rimpoche, and the thousands of bundles of scripts all carefully protected in brocade cloth wraps. These form a library and are catalogued in astrology, philosophy, and the various masters such as Nagarjuna, Tsongkapa, Atisha *etc*. dating back eighteen hundred years and more. They form a complex and indisputably advanced process of thinking and understanding of the true nature of our reality that even modern scientists appreciate as unique and so advanced. It is quite often beyond even their

grasp. I sit absorbed in thought, casually watching the stream of people turning the prayer wheels.

I become aware of an old woman, no more than 5ft tall, bent almost double with age, gnarled hands gripping the walking cane that supports her. Her clothes are dirty and torn; a thick pair of woollen socks preventing damage to her misshapen feet on which she wears old open toe sandals. Despite the warm weather she is obviously wearing many layers, and a woollen hat barely hiding the fact that she has very little hair. She has reached the end of the first row of wheels, and is chatting to two older women. Much gesticulating is going on but every now and again, she catches my eye—time for some camera work. I start shooting. I can see she is very alert as to what I am doing. She finishes her chat and instead of proceeding, as one should, to the next row of wheels, she goes back to the start. As she progresses, turning each one slowly, she makes sure I am taking photographs. Again, she reaches the end and once more restarts. This happens a third time and now she comes over to my bench and sits down. She has pieces of ancient turquoise and coral around her neck and an old gold ring on one finger of hands that seem almost fixed in a claw-like position. She chats to two young girls who have arrived, to what seems to me, to pay their respects. Not once yet have our eyes met. I can feel her body heat exuding out from the layers of woollen clothes. Suddenly she looks at me face on with a big smile from an almost toothless mouth. She starts to chat to me, although I can't understand any of what she is saying. A well-dressed Indian family is standing opposite watching us. The boy in his teens comes over and he too pays his respects and hands her a 50 rupee note, which she tucks, alongside a few others into the front of the old jacket. I point to my camera, "*tho che chey*", thank you in Tibetan, and hand her a 100 rupee bill. It disappears into the jacket along with the others. The Indian woman comes over and engages the old woman in conversation, then turns to me. "My name is Ruby, pleased to meet you. I can translate for you if you would like". She tells me the old girl is in her eighties and her husband died some 10 years back. Since then she has been sleeping and living rough, her home, apparently, a makeshift affair of old tarpaulins located in the cemetery. I feel myself well up with sadness that after being one of the first to cross the Himalayas on foot, that she should end up living in this appalling condition. I never did discover her importance or why people held her in such esteem, maybe it was simply because she is a survivor. Ruby carries on asking questions about me, relaying the answers to my newly made friend, who continues to hold me in her gaze, giving periodic toothless grins. The interview over, she heaves herself up, positions her cane, steadies her balance, and carries on her way. The backward look and another smile is something I will always remember. Ruby decides that this is now the time to bid farewell, with a shake of hands her comment is also one that I will not forget, "I am sure we have not met by accident, and I am sure we will meet again, goodbye."

The day has turned out to be quite an event. It is getting late as I head back. I am feeling an accomplished walker as the long upward hill walk from the temple has certainly done something toward my training for Tibet. The sky is unusually dark. The air seems to have a chill about it. Without warning a great gust of wind nearly knocks me off my feet. The sky is darkening even more. The stall holders are frantically packing up, a sense of unexplained urgency travels through the air with the wind picking up pace once again. I

increase my pace and reach the Moonpeak cafe just as all hell breaks loose. Hail the size of golf balls accompany the now nearly gale force wind. I dive into the cafe, then wish I hadn't as I watch through the windows at the struggle of the stall holders to keep control of their bits of plastic sheeting and tarpaulins that are held up with long sticks. These arrangements form the only protection of their livelihood. The scene reminds me of part of the film, *Mary Poppins*, when a huge and mysterious wind lifts all the people, by their umbrellas, off the ground. Bodies rotating being flung this way and that, like giant kites. Thankfully the folk here are staying on terra firma, but I see the street is hosting a surreal gravity free show of paper—prayer flags that have broken loose and an assortment of bits of stall, hats, telephone and electric wiring, and anything else this wind can detach from either the ground or its owners. Suddenly the door of the cafe bursts open, a tall Tibetan woman dragging a huge leather holdall is almost blown in. A young man rushes to her aid; she thanks him. A large straw hat is pulled firmly down on her head, but I think, judging from what little I can see of her features, that she has the long straight face of those from the Kham region of Tibet. She takes a seat by the window, her back is to me. We are both watching the scene outside.

With no apparent explanation I am now seeing a different scene. The hail is gone; pictures of wide valleys dotted with shapes that I cannot determine; mountains leave their shadows across green plains. A sense of calm and stability moves with the light breeze. I have no questions in my mind; there is no analysis or concern for where I am; the whole land is smiling and I smile back. I have no idea of the time span involved; it could be a few seconds or a few hours that I am held in this place. I am now aware that the woman is standing at the cafe door. She opens it, looks back at me and, with a single wave of her hand, is gone into the wind. Her leather holdall is nowhere to be seen. I am compelled instantly to put pen to paper. I open my note book and the words just flow. The verse and subsequent second verse that I write are at the end of this journal, titled "Verse for Tibet".

I spend all of this evening sitting on my little balcony, the prayer flags fluttering in the now gentle breeze. They remind me of the woman's hand, both generating the music and images of Tibet, but as I am about to discover, a Tibet that is now so very different. I can see the temple from where I am sitting, and can just make out the prayer wheels that are continuously rotating. The copper of the wheels catches the late sunset and throws out shafts of white light across the valley that separates the Pema Thang from the hill on which the Temple is built. Behind, and higher still, I can see the top floor and roof of The Dalai Lama's residence, perhaps knowing that he is here is why I have spent hours gazing across at this building in meditation.

WEDNESDAY MAY 20TH

Today is my last complete day here and I plan to spend it at the Norbulingka Institute. I am up early for breakfast. I spot the German lady coming into the restaurant, the first I have seen of her since the tweezers incident. I give her a smile, and am surprised to have my acknowledgment returned. Usually she makes a point of eating on her own so

I am even more surprised when she asks if she can join me. I decide not to mention the dog or the tweezers, that event is gone and past. Her personality seems to have changed somewhat and she is quite relaxed as we chat about the fact this is my last day. She has a further week before returning to Germany. I discover that she has attended a residential 10 course studying *Tushita*, a form of Buddhist philosophy and meditation, and that she is a yoga teacher in Germany. Determined that I should not spend the last day on my own, she invites herself to accompany me to the Norbulingka.

What to do? I so want to go on my own but here the woman is obviously trying to make some sort of reconciliation. However the difficulty of pairing up is soon obvious. She has not travelled on local transport, preferring the safety, as she sees it, of going everywhere by taxi—very expensive. Indeed, she flew here from Delhi, rather than take the train or bus. I explain that my budget, with still a lot of travel to do, does not accommodate taxis. "You will be fine on the bus it is only about 40 minutes and is only 15 rupees compared to 600 rupees, which split still is 300 each." My assurances are not penetrating the woman's rather inflexible attitude. Finally she agrees. I was hoping that she might decide to give the idea a miss and I can then have the day to myself. She needs time to prepare, we agree to meet in 30 minutes at 9.30 outside Sonam's office. My preparation involves nothing more than grabbing my camera, notebook, and some money. I chat to Sonam in his office as I wait, we are in deep conversation about Mahamudra meditation, causing me to lose track of time. The door bursts open, a very irate travelling companion is waving her arms pointing at the time and shouting "we go NOW, we go NOW, it will be too hot if we don't go NOW, please we go NOW. She is dressed for a major expedition, hiking boots, backpack, walking sticks, 2 different hats, sunglasses, guide books and I don't know what else! I can't help but cast a glance at myself—cotton singlet which, after I bought it from an Indian trader, I discovered is printed with salutations to Hare Krishna—very unfortunate, but the thing is so comfortable I still wear it; long cotton pants, pockets bulging with the few necessities for the day, and jandals—finish! Now I am not an authority on yoga, but my little understanding is that calm is a necessity to practice correctly. For the 2nd time I am witnessing quite the opposite in this lady who is now pacing up and down outside Sonam's office. He gives me a look of sympathy, knowing that I am about to embark on a day with her. I can't do it. Lie if I must but my last day in this woman's company—no! "I'm sorry to have kept you waiting, I was consulting Sonam about the best remedy for Delhi belly, I really don't think I should risk going to far after all. You go on and maybe I will catch you up later in the day" Any deity that maybe listening I am hoping will forgive my story! I watch her steam off down the hill hoping that any deity that may be watching may instruct her in the art of patience and tolerance. I do feel sad for the lady. She has come all this way to increase her depth of understanding of a subject and yet seems to have actually learned very little. I return to my room to wait half an hour before starting my day. At least I know I am safe on public transport as the woman, if she carries on with our plan, will take a taxi.

One of the things that is so enjoyable about the bus, certainly not the suspension, is the amazing array of people. Women, in their brightly coloured saris, usually with at least two children equally colourful; Students, laden down with files and books, and quite often plugged into a personal stereo or some such device; Monks in their red and yellow

robes; Westerners in their usual attire of well-worn hippy gear and always with the great array of trinket adornments that jingle, tinkle, jangle in perpetual motion; all mingle with bags of vegetables, fruit and sundry items bulging out from the top. I leave the bus at the bottom of the hill once again and look round for a share jeep—none to be seen; well the walk is all good training.

As I enter the Norbulingka, which is named after the Dalai Lama's summer residence in Tibet, the serenity and tranquility is almost tangible. The reception is shaped like a T—the long upright part hosting a dazzling collection of original statues of the various deities including the 21 Taras—the White Tara being a very important part of Tibetan culture. The two horizontal areas house an Aladdin's cave of the most exquisitely painted and appliqué Thankas, some, at an estimate, 6 feet in length. These take years to complete by the Thanka masters and with so few of them left now, the work here to teach this art is invaluable. I have heard that Americans will wait 10 years for one of these done by a certain master.

Exiting reception, I enter a wonderful garden. Stone paths meander through leafy glades; prayer flags flutter, casting their shadow across the water of the ornate ponds. The route to the temple takes me over more large ponds via a bridge beautifully decorated in Tibetan style. The surface of the water is broken with dozens of beautiful water lilies. Out from the murky bottom and the mud come these amazing flowers, a very auspicious symbol in Buddhist philosophy. Large koi carp glide past. There is no sound other than that of the birds. All in all an ambience that instantly leaves me feeling that I too am just gliding in this wonderful place. I feel a familiarity about being here and puzzle over why, and then it dawns on me. This is where Michael Palin did some of his Himalaya film for the BBC, one of his interviews was held right here on this bridge. The Temple is obviously the main focal point, and within, the centerpiece is a magnificent 14 ft high image of Shakyamuni gilded in copper. The walls are covered in the various scenes from Buddhist and Tibetan history and one can hear a pin drop it is so quiet. There is only one other person—in deep meditation. I too now take time to bathe my mind in this serenity.

Feeling very refreshed, my wanderings now take me to the Losel Doll Museum. I pay the 50 rupee entrance to this tiny place that houses exquisitely hand made *papier maché* figures all in Tibetan costume depicting either the various regions—Amdo, Kham, Utsang, Ngari, or a few of the many festival scenes that used to be commonplace in Tibet and, which I have heard, are no more. The scenes are displayed as a story of Tibet before the tragedies of the last 50 years. These miniature scenes are so valuable for preserving the detail of Tibetan life along with the skill needed to make these exquisite figures.

Once back outside it is not difficult to locate the small café that is now hosting a very large Indian family busy ordering an equally large lunch. I find a quiet spot under the trees trying not to be too obvious in the fact that I am being entertained by the family opposite. Their dishes start to arrive; every available staff member seems to be engaged in this task as the mountain of food just keeps on coming. I think they have ordered everything on the menu!

After a sweet lassi, I locate the Institute shop, this time without my American friend. I

admire the quality of everything, from hand carved wooden altars and tables, down to sheets of hand made silk paper. I notice a print of the Dalai Lama and his family from the fifties, before they left Tibet, a nice gift for Matthew and Lucy. It is a limited edition on beautifully made card, large enough to be framed and hung. Attached to the shop is a workshop. Young Tibetans are busy learning all the traditional skills to keep their art and culture alive. I watch for some time, amazed by the dedication of ones so young, with such basic facilities and tools. As I turn to leave I see the large Indian family from the café. My attention drawn to one of the young women, no more than 5ft tall, has both legs in calipers—the old fashioned kind that one rarely sees now in the West. I catch her eye with a smile which is instantly returned.

Time now to locate the Dolma Ling nunnery which I believe is located somewhere at the back of the complex. An old, rusty gate, almost hidden by overgrown foliage, is tucked away in a corner of the huge perimeter wall. With some force it opens. I find myself out on a dusty track and not a lot else. The Himalayas stretch away in front of me; the air mass providing perfect gliding conditions for the small eagles that frequent this area. They epitomize the freedom that has been so cruelly taken from the Tibetan people. I watch them circling, waiting for the moment they spot something to sustain their life. The heat is oppressive as I make my way uphill toward a cluster of houses. There is no one to ask if I am heading in the right direction, the houses seem quite deserted. I take a different track back to Norbulingka and stumble, almost literally, on a tiny chai, or tea, shack. A tiny table and one chair sit in the dust, and, as can only happen somewhere like this, it is a billiard table that has seen better days, but is hosting an intense game judging by the amount of shouting and arm waving. The proprietor is obviously engaged in the game rather than tea making, but the chair offers some relief for my tired legs.

"Would you like some tea" a broad Welsh accent from behind me gives me a fright. An older man, obviously well travelled by his appearance and with a beaming grin grabs my hand and gives it a firm shake. "Hi I am Lindsay, tea or a smoke?"

"I'll settle for tea thanks, I give the smoke a miss these days" is my somewhat flustered answer. He disappears into the hut, and is back in no time with hot cinnamon tea. He then proceeds to pile a heap of ganga into a cigarette paper, lights up and blows a mouthful of smoke at me. Well like it or not I guess I am going to get a taste of Indian ganga! Without stopping for breath, other than to keep puffing away, I get his complete life story in about 10 minutes, which is the best thing for me as I would have been too dopey to make it back! He is a character from the past, one that never went home. Fluent in Tibetan and Nepali, having done more things than I would have thought humanly possible, he has, for the past 6 months, been living in the Dolma Ling nunnery, gratis, in return for some Welsh cooking lessons, English lessons and general maintenance. He also teaches in the local school three mornings a week. He is full of life and laughter and remarks on the empty houses that I came across. "No they are not empty. Western students live reclusive lives there. Just study Buddhist philosophy and stuff. They hardly ever show, can't see the point in it. There is no giving or being part of what is here, but they think they're on the right track." I reflect on some of the moments I have had in McCleod Ganj that echo his sentiments. "Well nice meeting you Mrs. Jane, have the trip you dreamed of in Tibet, adios" and he is gone.

The Norbulingka is beginning to close by the time I get back. After a swift descent down the hill to the main road, I locate the bus stop and wait, and wait and wait! A share jeep comes into view and I flag it down. The driver waves me to get into a non existent space, which I do, and sit on a young Indian student's lap! I am next to a very large western woman who, I would say, was in her late forties. She is having trouble with the heat by the looks of her ruddy complexion and the perspiration running from every pore. What I was not prepared for was the next 40 minutes of verbal siege that I am now being subjected to with what seems like only two pauses for breath.

"Hi I'm Margaret—from Manchester originally, now semi permanent resident here and there, where ever there is a cause worth standing up for." And so it went on and on and on. Apparently she is on a disability benefit from the UK Government after a car crash some six years earlier. Now in India with her teenage daughter, who by all accounts is a budding artist and has been commissioned to do a portrait for some local Raja in return for board and lodging for the pair of them. I can feel my eyebrows rise steadily as I try desperately to keep a straight face. She goes on for a while about the crash, then a business card is thrust into my face. SAVE THE PLANET support the trees. All donations to Margaret at a Post Office Box number.

"I have an audience with the Karmapa, he is right behind this. His support will do wonders" I wonder if the Karmapa knows about this. We finally arrive in McCleod Ganj. I pay my share—15 rupees—of the fare, bid farewell and every success to Margaret, and once out of her sight absolutely crack up laughing. I am almost on my knees, I just cannot stop laughing and now causing others to look, probably thinking I have overdone the ganja! By the time I arrive at the Pema Thang my ribs are painful with laughter and the squeeze of the jeep ride plus a bear hug of a farewell from Margaret. I am hot, sweaty and tired. Sonam who spots me probably thought I would have returned in better shape had I been in the company of the organized German woman. I have to add at this point, that some months after my return to New Zealand I read an article by The Karmapa, endorsing a local scheme to prevent any further forest removal in the Himachal Pradesh region. Good on you, Margaret!

This is my last evening here at the Pema Thang, and it is tinged with a little sadness as I order dinner. Suddenly from behind, in a very English accent comes "Boy, I say boy, clear these plates" Every hair on the back of my neck stands to attention. The young lad who serves all the tables from morning to night looks across. He is a refugee and has been sent by his family, now in Sikkim, to earn a living here at the guesthouse owned by his Aunt. He is probably about 20 years of age and only just managing the language problem as well as the workload. The voice from behind comes again, this time louder and with increased irritation. The lad rushes over and is clearing the table when a heated discussion starts about bread. Evidently they had wanted more with their meal, which had not been forthcoming. I can hear him try to explain that there was no more, but they persist. Well that has done it! I spin round and confront two girls, teenagers I would say, who are bedecked in so many Buddhist trinkets, from mala beads to coral and turquoise that they look quite ridiculous. To top it off they have their designer sunglasses perched on top heads, and the mobile phones and laptops to complete the picture. "Firstly, he is not boy, he has a name. I think you will find that only so much

bread can be served with a meal, to ensure there is enough for breakfast. Secondly, if you watch, you will see that many of the people here take their used plates to the hatch on their way out, this is helpful to Tenzin who has to do everything here solo." There is a long silence. I catch Tenzin's cheeky face, sporting an ear-to-ear grin, peeking out from behind the kitchen door. The girls resume their conversation on a different topic, but nonetheless as infuriating.

"My room is so Buddhist is yours?"

"I think that Guru so and so is really cool, he told me I am so Tibetan."

I collect up my used crockery and head for the door, enough is enough!! Time to start packing for the trip back to Delhi tomorrow. The empty suitcase I brought is going to be full.

As I pack I reflect on the two girls in the restaurant. They bring me to the thoughts of the introduction from Professor Robert Thurman in The Dalai Lama's teaching *The Blade Wheel of Mind Transformation*. In it he states that people study a little bit and believe they have found a little realisation, this can lead to the imagination believing that one has found a bit more until finally one can convince oneself that one has found nirvana or enlightenment. The blade wheel acts as a tool to cut through the ego that leads, in many cases, to this delusion that enlightenment is obtained in ten short lessons.

The twinkling lights of McCleod Ganj seem to be a reflection of the million stars that fill the clear sky. The last 10 days have not been what I had expected; they have been very much more. Some profound moments intermingled with laughter, smiles and a deep sense that I do have a connection with the Tibetan people.

THURSDAY MAY 21ST

I am up bright and early and take my bags to Sonam's office. He looks at the increased amount of luggage and advises a taxi down to the bus station rather than the long legged porter. I have until 5pm; all the farewells I have planned will probably take up most of that time.

I start off downhill toward the main Namgyal Temple, call into the Moonpeak café, then find the locks lady who thrusts a little parcel into my hand whilst quietly talking in Tibetan. Her eyes are filled with tears as are mine. All I can say is '*tho che chey*' and '*Tashi delek*'—'thank you' and 'goodbye'. I do not open the parcel of paper, but put it I my pocket for later. I meet the Israeli butter lamp lady at the Temple entrance. "I go back to Delhi today so I'm glad I have seen you to say goodbye and thank you, His Holiness did bless the things I am taking with me to Tibet"

"Don't forget to take altitude sickness tablets, get them in Nepal, Diamox, remember. I have something else for you to take, give them to the people in Lhasa, but do it carefully" She gives me an envelope, inside a small quantity of minute red beads. "They are mani pills,

made from barley flour and water and blessed by His Holiness. It is a signal that they are not forgotten and that he has them in his heart. By swallowing them his blessings are absorbed into the body." With that she is gone.

I carry on to the Temple, complete the kora and go inside for the last time. The great gleaming image of Shakyamuni looks me straight in the eye, filling my heart with peace and a sort of confidence. I have my trip to Tibet very much in the front of my mind. The Great Buddha knows this. Surrounded by the images of Guru Rimpoche and Chenrezig, his thousand arms, needed to embrace all of Tibet and bring them into the spirit of Buddha thousands of years ago, fan out around his body. The Kalachakra temple and the Wheel of Time is the area I have always found myself drawn to during my visits here, today it is filled with energy.

I go out into the morning sun, find a seat, and open the first of my two little packages—the tiny pills in the envelope. A people torn in two by the Chinese will face arrest if found with these and yet they risk that happily. What place have we, as human beings, reached, that a person could suffer such brutality just for a pill no bigger than a small bead? And that this bead is all they have left to stay in touch with their spiritual leader The Dalai Lama, Ocean of Wisdom, as his title translates. I close the envelope and carefully tuck it into my wallet. The second package reveals a beautiful coral and turquoise bracelet and two old Tibetan coins. I stare in disbelief as the tears, once again, roll down my face. How could the lady of locks have known the one thing that captured my heart during my visit to Tibet House in Delhi, was the little cabinet containing Tibetan money.

I leave the Temple for the last time, but before I leave the complex I notice that the little museum is now open. It has been closed until today, very auspicious I think, to find it open on my last day. I pay the entrance and find myself looking at the history of the Tibetan people in exile, told in an array of huge photographs. The photo I keep returning to is that of the Dalai Lama outside his first residence, no more than a shack, greeting a handful of newly arrived refugees. They are standing in a sea of mud. His robes are torn and his shoes are barely visible in the mud. The expression on his face is pure compassion as he talks to the ragtag group of people in front of him. I leave the photo area and find myself confronted with displays of images of the beatings and killings that have been smuggled out. A blood soaked shirt lies alongside some of the tools of torture used on the many hundreds of thousands of prisoners still held. The reality check is overpowering, seeing these things right here in front of me. I discover that many exhibits are not yet on display as the museum has just returned from a tour and the unpacking is still in progress. I have seen enough of the stark reminders as to the truth of what is still happening behind the Chinese statement "there is no Tibetan problem". I wonder if Palden Gyatso, held for 33 years, whose book *Fire Under the Snow*, graphically detailing those years, would agree. One can wipe away the tears from the eyes, but how does one dry the tears that pour from the heart? All this fills my mind as I turn away. On the way out I collect an armful of pamphlets including a booklet about the workings of the Kashag, the Tibetan Government, all of which will have to stay in Nepal as they cannot be taken into Tibet.

Back at the Pema Thang it is time for more farewells and I load up the waiting taxi. Sonam, who has always been rather quiet, takes my hand, "we hope you come back, next

time you can volunteer your services at the vets". All the kitchen and restaurant staff says lots of things in Tibetan accompanied by wide smiles. Then I see Jacqui, she is flying back to Delhi tomorrow, then back to Holland. I am encased in a bear hug. "Be safe in Tibet, no risks please, don't forget to email your report to Karma when you get back to New Zealand, maybe we will meet again one day" She is gone before I have chance to reply.

The bus station is very busy and it is down to trial and error to ensure I find the right one. I choose a window seat, hopefully I will not have the same battles that I had coming from Pathankot. There is not much leg room and nowhere for hand luggage. The air conditioning turns out to be a small desk fan screwed to the interior above my head, the wires of which dangle aimlessly! A monk takes the seat in front of me, then wallop! he lowers the back into the sleeping position, literally, and I am left looking at the top of his head which, to all intents and purposes is now in my lap! Oh happy days! I muse for a moment. Why me? Why does a baboon pick on me, why did I have such trouble with the Delhi metro, why did I have to find the ticks on the dog, why do I have a monk's head in my lap for the next 13 hours! My only solace is that it is faster than the train and I am glad I did not book the economy coach!

It is 10.30pm and we have finally stopped for a break. My head is thumping with the headache of all headaches and the problem I have been having with an ear infection is back with vengeance. I have no feeling in my legs and I so wish, at this moment, I was on a beach in Fiji. I wait until everyone has left the bus then peel my butt from the plastic seat. I wait for 5 minutes for the circulation to return to my legs before I stagger off to find a cup of tea and the ladies. I am now at the back of the queue for everything, by the time it is my turn for the toilet, which does have a seat, any thoughts or food immediately vanish. I only just pay for a tea when the hooter on the bus sounds, the call for all to return. The why me syndrome has returned! The seat next to me, which has been occupied by a very quiet student, is now taken by a large Indian woman who only adds to my discomfort. As we leave the town the main highway which has been good up to now, seems to be missing a sealed surface. We pass miles of resurfacing trucks that are busy working through the night. Every bone in my body is being shaken and bounced. The monk's horizontal seat is almost being flung off its bolts but he appears to be sleeping through it all. This is a nightmare! It is now 2.30am and we have stopped for another break, this time in a truckers' park rather than a hotel. There are sleeping bodies everywhere, some on mattresses, others just curled up under their truck. The heat is stifling; there are clouds of flies following packs of rangy mongrels, if one of them is fortunate to find a scrap of food, a fight then follows. Despite the pain I push my way off the bus desperate to find some bottled water in order to finish the last of my pain killers, and smoke as many cigarettes as possible without being sick!

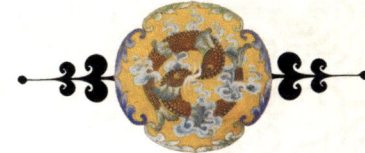

FRIDAY MAY 22ND

At last we enter the city suburbs. It is 7.30am and the frenzy of Delhi rush-hour delays our arrival at the bus depot. By now I really don't care. A flurry of tuktuks looking for fares descend on the passengers as they alight. I grab my bags and the nearest ride. "Can I

share with you" a voice from behind in a broad American accent. "Where are you going" is my tired reply. "I'll just get off when you do" is the vague answer. I am too tired and irritable to argue. The lady ends up sitting on my bags and carries on chatting. I cannot register any of what she is saying. When we arrive at the Yatri I discover she has no money for her share of the cost and she disappears into the multitudes that are on their way to work. The houseboy is there to greet me and takes me directly to my room, no waiting this time. Within 5 minutes a breakfast tray arrives and I am left in peace to recover from my journey.

SATURDAY MAY 23RD

The following morning the stresses and strains of the previous two days have evaporated with a night's sleep in a comfortable bed. I am sitting opposite a tall middle aged European man, about to consume a large breakfast. He looks over the top of his paper and bids me good morning in an American accent. I am too preoccupied with the thoughts of my flight to Nepal that leaves in 4 hours to engage in conversation. However, he persists as my breakfast arrives.

"Is this your first trip to India" he enquires.

"No I was here in 1972 and 73, much has changed, how about you, have you visited before?"

"Yes, my wife and I came in 1990", then a story unfolds, the like of which one usually reads in a magazine. My thoughts of Nepal cast aside for the next 20 minutes. He and his wife had gone to Calcutta, with the express purpose of adopting a child, I think from Mother Theresa's orphanage. They adopted a baby girl and had gone back to America. Evidently they had promised that once the child reached the age of 18, they would return with her to meet her family, if she so wished. He talked on about the problems she had had with colour and her short stature, and now back in India had remarked to her father that he was now the wrong colour and too tall! I can sense emotions are already running high with this venture and I wish he and his daughter the happiest of conclusions possible with the reuniting of her true family.

The morning seems to be getting busier as I now have Sanjay Puri, the proprietor sitting at my little table, immersed in trying to stop an army of ants invading the sugar. Suddenly there is a kafuffle in the corridor that divides the back courtyard, where we are sitting, and the front of the guesthouse. I can hear a woman's voice with a French accent reaching a crescendo and glimpse rapid arm waving. Sanjay is on his feet, but does not appear to be easing the trouble.

"I expect a discount and a courtesy car" the lady is shouting. "Madam, there is no discount for 5 days stay and the courtesy car is booked, please, your taxi is waiting" With that her bags are firmly dumped at her feet and she is left to haul them to the waiting car, whose driver is equally reluctant to help. I have taken this opportunity to assemble my luggage in readiness for the journey to the airport which, with time pressing, I am keen to get underway.

I had expected Sanjay to organize a taxi, but to my absolute surprise my bags are being loaded into the courtesy car. "I hope you enjoyed your stay, madam, it would be helpful if the Yatri were to be put in the top ten best places to stay in the Independent Travellers Guide. We are currently listed number 16—a slightly unfair rating I think. Please have a pleasant flight to Nepal, the driver will take you to the International departure and guide you through security. Hope we see you again."

As I leave the city behind, I muse on Sanjay's parting comments, somewhat mystified by them. Then, a moment of realization; he has seen me scribbling away in my notebook, and taking photos of the guesthouse and courtyard, maybe he has thought I am connected to the travel guide he mentioned, perhaps he was expecting a visit. That explains the upgrade in service generally and the car to the airport. Well Sanjay, I am afraid I don't work in the travel industry, but the following few sentences are for you.

The Yatri Guesthouse. An old established, family run, guesthouse located in a quiet leafy cul-de-sac just two metro stops from Connaught Circus. Well appointed rooms with private bathrooms, tea and coffee making facilities. Breakfast included in the competitive room rate, and courtesy car to the airport or railway station, if available. Highly recommended.

We arrive at the airport and, oh! my goodness it is busy. Soldiers, with weapons, are everywhere, keeping the hundreds of non flying friends and family of those who are going somewhere away from the terminal entrance. I join the long queue passing through two vigorous security checks where I finally lose my lighter! I see it join dozens of others in a large box. I'm sure they are making a fortune reselling them! The political tensions and terrorist threats are obvious. In the early seventies, when I was last here, I traveled overland from London to Kathmandu, and remember sitting on a border, I think between Afghanistan and Pakistan, for nearly two days until some one was found to stamp the passports! Things are sadly different these days.

I don't have to wait long before the flight to Nepal is called. I have a window seat in anticipation of the sky being clear enough to see the tops of the Himalayas. As we taxi down the runway I wonder if I will see India again—certainly not if I have to wait another 37 years! The flight is only just over an hour in duration and I wait for the view that I have been hoping for. Suddenly, through light cloud, I can see them, the snow covered peaks of the Himalayas—it is a wonderful sight. I am joined by a little Indian girl, evidently on her first flight, and being stuck in an aisle seat, had decided I could be an accommodating lap to get the view. She is probably no more than 5 or 6 years, I am as excited as my new friend, as we peer through the small porthole upon the frozen majesty of nature.

Residence of the Karmapa. Sidhibari

Main Street. Mcleod Gan

Friend from Ladakh

Lady at the Temple

Refugee children

Lady of the locks.

Sunset. Mcleod Ganj

Mcleod Ganj

Mcleod Ganj

Prayer flags. Norbulingka

Norbulingka Institute

NEPAL
MAY 23RD–MAY 28TH

TRIBHUVAN AIRPORT. KATHMANDU. NEPAL SAT. MAY 23rd

The first effects on air passengers of the swine flu epidemic that is, by all accounts, global are being felt here. There are long queues to complete health information forms and the detailing of one's movements before arriving and during a stay in Nepal. I am still bogged down in reams of red tape two hours after touchdown. Finally I get to the visa desk, complete more forms, pay the fee and locate the baggage carousel. I am praying that the Hotel Utse, which I have prebooked, has sent a car and that the driver has been informed as to reasons for the long wait. The temperature is noticeably cooler as I step out into Nepal and see a sign bearing my name, stuck to the forehead of a young Nepali. He immediately grabs my bags and takes off at a brisk pace through a sea of parked cars and buses. Once again I hardly recognize anything. Everything is so modern compared to the days when this was known as the Himalayan Kingdom of Nepal, and considered quite an adventure to come here.

The Hotel Utse is located in Jyaira Thamel, a low budget area, full of tourist shops but I notice not many tourists. The interior is furnished very much in Tibetan style, but the place has obviously seen better days. I am greeted by a rather morose Nepali manager, and shown into a drab room, with the only window looking straight into a brick wall of the apartment block next door. I am not a happy bunny! I go back to reception and insist that the Hotels description of a superior grade room cannot be the room allocated to me.

Finally I get another room with a television and a view of the street down below, slightly better than a brick wall! Already I feel on edge.

There is a tension in Kathmandu that I can't describe and the air is heavy with it. I have two days here on my own before I move to the Radisson Hotel and join the group which will take me to Tibet. I can feel my impatience building up as I am now so close to my real goal. As twilight descends I hear the street below beginning to buzz with the youth of Kathmandu starting their Saturday night revelling. The traffic is chaotic with motorbikes, bicycles many with the rickshaw attached, cars, most of which are the Land Cruiser type, and folk on foot trying to weave their way in and out of the mayhem without getting killed. I am not going to get much sleep tonight! The hotel seems almost deserted as I wander back, down the three flights of stairs, to locate the restaurant. The walls are festooned with memorabilia from climbing expeditions dating back to the early 60s with some photos of Tibet including one of the Potala and a couple of unnamed monasteries. It all looks rather sad and faded, from an era when the Beatles, the Rolling Stones, Guru Maharishi and the like, when peace and love was being felt around the world, and where places like Kathmandu and the Hotel Utse became one of the global hubs for a change in international policies towards war, famine, and human rights. The clear vision may have been a little obscured by incense and marijuana, but these days so many care for nothing at all, their vision clouded by ecstasy and methamphetamine, computer games that challenge the individual to wreak as much carnage as possible in five minutes and win points for doing it. Cynics of those days tag them as being one of the reasons we have ended up where we are today. I would suggest that they should look at those who did not have, at least a taste, of that culture. When I had come here in 1972, the hippy era was coming to an end, and my intention was not so much to be part of "the following" as I already had a deep interest in Tibet and Buddhism, but I had intended to purchase a sitar. The Buddhist reason flourished, the sitar never materialized! I was just under 18 and my father had taken me to court in order to try and stop the venture by having me made a ward of court—which was rather extreme!

The restaurant and lobby are devoid of guests and staff, but having cast a glance outside, and seen the groups of young men, mostly intoxicated, hanging round, I decide to stay where I am. I find the kitchen and an elderly man asleep in a chair. Several loud coughs finally wake him and after some prompting he agrees to supply some soup. I am having mixed feelings as to whether to continue staying here, or to find an alternative for the remaining two nights. Will give it more thought in the morning.

SUNDAY MAY 24TH

It is pouring with rain, the first I have seen since the storm on McCleod Ganj. The gutters are overflowing due to large amounts of rubbish that form piles in the street. All of the little stalls and shops that I can see from the Utse's entrance are closed, and the groups of men still seem to be here, hanging around in doorways to avoid the weather. That feeling of tension is back, I have not seen one smiling face. Dodging the traffic seems to be an art. I find a coffee shop and wait for the rain to stop, a pointless exercise as it becomes

clear this is set for the day. I go over the street map acquired at the airport, and try to make some plan in order not to waste the day. The Dream Gardens and the Royal Palace, Swayambunath or the monkey temple as it used to be nicknamed are all places on my list and only two days to do them. A bumpy bike rickshaw ride takes me to Dream Gardens only to find it closed. I ask about the piles of rubbish that are everywhere. "There is a strike, no rubbish collection, because of the Government problems" is the answer.

I am dropped off in Durbar Square, one of the most famous landmarks in the city which, despite the rain, is bustling with activity. The first construction of "the heart of Kathmandu" started in 1069 and is steeped in the history of Kings and Gods from the Hindu faith. Age and the environment have meant extensive renovation work over the decades and Durbar Square is now a World Heritage site. One of the most famous parts is the Kumari chok; the Kumari being a young virgin who remains inside her temple and on certain festival days, which I am unfamiliar with, shows her face from one of the tiny windows. This practice currently continues. I try to locate some of the areas I remember, it is all so different. Amazingly, the small kitchen that is tucked away in one of the few original parts is still here. Memories of coming here early in the morning to buy bread and hot milk come flooding back. The big cauldron is still bubbling, but the milk seems to have been replaced with rice and travelers by locals.

I have a feeling that I am being followed, a young Nepali seems to be constantly behind me. I stop, look around, sure enough, he is there. This time I walk over.

"Is there a reason you seem to be behind me all the time,"

"Yes Madam I am your guide for the day, I will take you to all the places and explain their history"

"Well if you are a guide, shouldn't you be in front. I am sorry, I didn't book a guide, and I do know my way around, thank you anyway, but no thank you"

This young man is obviously used to dealing with no thank yous and persists. I can feel the irritation building up. Finally he suggests we go for coffee in one of the rooftop cafés and discuss the possibility I may change my mind. Well I could do with a coffee, the view is probably spectacular, and I could do with getting out of the rain that has subsided to a drizzle. The long climb up countless steps is worth it. The view over the Kathmandu valley is amazing but, alas, so much is now under concrete. Houses stretch as far as the eye can see. I pick out the huge stupas of Swayambunath and Boudinath, with the mountains as their backdrop, and begin to relax. He seems a nice enough young man and is more interested in what I can tell him about Kathmandu all those years ago, long before he was born. We touch on the subject of the Tibetans that use Nepal as a crossing point out of Tibet. There used to be a large centre here for those new arrivals but the Nepalese Government, now Maoist, has recently closed it down. He is not sympathetic with the Tibetan cause, and regards the refugees that are here as troublemakers. I keep my opinions low key as this is a very political young man, and very much a Maoist. Time to part company, so with a promise that I will return tomorrow with a view to possibly taking a motorbike ride to the ancient town of Patan I leave him with his thoughts of how the radical new Government is going to change things. I think they need to start by getting the enormous piles of refuse off the streets and

putting an end to the strike!

I get quite lost walking back to the hotel in the maze of alleys and cut-throughs. Some of the old buildings survive, but they are in very poor shape, many uninhabited as the decay continues to ravage the old city. The air is thick with the stench of rotting rubbish, and smoke. People are now igniting the problem as their frustration with many empty promises to clean up boils over. Back at the Utse, the atmosphere has not improved, I have decided that it is not worth moving as I check in at the Radisson on Tuesday, however I will find an alternative for the four days I have after Tibet and before I return to New Zealand.

MONDAY MAY 25TH

I have found a coffee shop that does wonderful breakfast pancakes, and a pharmacy to stock up on the altitude sickness pills Diamox, as suggested by the Israeli butter lamp woman. The weather has cleared so today I am off to Swayambunath to the climb of 365 stone steps, which should be a test for Tibet. The temperature is a cool 32°F and I am enjoying the walk down to the river. As I approach the bridge I can already detect an increase in the stench of rotting rubbish. The river has very little water but the refuse is mountainous. For the first time I see men women and children, scouring the piles of garbage, collecting anything that might be of some value. I do not recollect these scenes of desperation in the 70s, maybe they were here and I simply didn't notice. As I approach

Swayambunath there are signs of the Tibetan community. It looks much run down but I expect the spirit is still here—one would hope so anyway.

The great stupa with the four pairs of eyes looking in the four directions, towers way above me. It is a long climb. Although the monkey population here seems to have declined, nonetheless there are a few mums with their young clinging on, as they race up and down the steps, scattering a few tourists in their wake. I have to stop for a break, with about half the distance covered, my age and questionable fitness beginning to tell. Kathmandu is at an altitude of 1400 meters above sea level, and combined with the increasing temperature of the day and stillness of the air, I am wondering if I will make it to the top. Finding the determination needed I continue, now counting the paces between brief stops. The last 30 or so steps are much narrower and almost vertical, but I have made it. The great gilded dorje, or thunderbolt, symbolizing the unity of wisdom and emptiness when accompanied by the vajra bell, greets the eye as does the enormity of the great stupa festooned in prayer flags. The views are breathtaking. Telescopes have been installed at strategic places but apart from that nothing much seems to have changed.

Buddhist history tells us that Kathmandu valley was once a great lake, with a single lotus flower growing in the centre. Manjushri, the deity of wisdom, cut through the surrounding mountains with his sword and the waters drained away leaving this fertile valley and the lotus which settled on top of a hill and was transformed into the stupa. There is no nose, The symbol below the eyes on the stupa is not a nose but is the Nepali number one, and represents the single path to enlightenment. The surrounding areas

of the site house many small shrines for different deities, and there is a Hindu temple dedicated to Haravati, protector against smallpox and other diseases. Its presence demonstrates the intermingling of Buddhism and Hinduism that goes back 2000 years. I follow the general flow of visitors down a long wide stone staircase and find myself in quite a new part, obviously an addition. There is a Buddha pool—not so sure I am taken with this—and a new information centre for the monkey population complete with their own bathing pool! I read some of the billboard-size notices warning tourists not to feed the monkeys as inappropriate diet has led to their decline in numbers. I keep walking only to find the crème-de-la-crème of extras for the wonderful tourists—those who have poisoned the monkeys—a new road that will bring them up here by taxi! Apparently it is only the pilgrims, monks and the dedicated fitness junkies that still use the traditional way of the steps. I wonder which category I fit in to?

I have spent the best part of 3 hours up here, turned the prayer wheels, completed the khora around the stupa, chatted to some monks and now begin the leisurely walk down.

On the return walk I try to locate the Delight Lodge, not the most up market of backpackers. My memory is somewhat hazy, but I do remember it being close to the river and my view was of the Stupa and one single tree. The alleys run in every direction possible and within 30 minutes I am very confused and completely lost. Distracted from my plight for a moment, I can hear children singing and locate the direction it is coming from. I peer through a very small window almost at street level, into what seems like a dungeon. It is a school classroom, the light almost nonexistent, but I make out a room full of small children, all in blue uniforms, sitting in the dust of the floor, singing their hearts out. There is a blackboard on the wall and, from what little I can see, not much else. My eyes well with tears as I watch the group, they have so little, but are singing their song with such passion. The song finishes, they all stand and bid, I guess, a courteous thank you and good afternoon to the departing teacher. A door beside me bursts open. It reminds me of a flock of bluebirds taking flight into the afternoon sun, their wings open and free. They dart past me, not noticing the stranger in their midst, except for two small boys who have spotted a potentially lucrative moment by stopping and attempting to engage me in conversation about their dire circumstances. I negotiate a deal with them to guide me back to the Hotel Utse in return for some things of their choice from the local grocery store, rather than cash, which is what they were hoping for. We chat about their aspirations for the future. One of them wants to be a lawyer, I so hope he makes it; he certainly is quick with cheeky response when it comes time to part company.

"You shouldn't beg for money, tourists don't like it" I say firmly.

"You no smoking Mrs. Very bad" is the response. Touché, he is right!

This is the last night here and I will not be sorry to change hotels in the morning. It has a decidedly hostile atmosphere with only one or two other guests. Tomorrow I also change from being a solo traveler to one of a group, a new experience for me and one that I am feeling a little apprehensive about.

TUESDAY MAY 26TH

I pull into the entrance of the Radisson Hotel in a battered old taxi. The door attendant tries to open the car door that has decided to stick fast. Whilst I scramble across the front seat a tooting of horns from behind start up. I give a backward glance to see a Mercedes and four-wheel-drives queuing up behind. The doorman can see my obvious embarrassment and gives me a helping hand, unloading the bags with the ever increasing, irritated queue being given no more than a cursory glance. This is a US$180 per night hotel as opposed to US$15 which was the average charged so far of my accommodation. I have stayed in many hotels worldwide in this bracket, the Hiltons, Sheratons *etc*, but all a long time ago. As I stand in the huge entrance, I am like a fish out of water. The tour company has a desk for registering their client's arrival. It is here that I learn my partner for the next 3 weeks is also from New Zealand and has already arrived. Next stop is reception to obtain my key, then to locate the lift as we are on the 4th floor. There are helpful staff everywhere which is just as well as I discover I have been standing outside the ladies toilet instead of the lift. The friendly bellboy escorts me to lifts without so much as a glimmer of what he is probably quietly thinking: "We have a right one here!"

The room is small but with all the accessories one would expect in this price range. A full-length window overlooks the front entrance with the Hotel Tibet to my left and a building site to my right—rather like Spain, without the ocean! My room buddy is not here but a book has been left on the one and only window seat and the luggage on the only stand. Now I am reminded of holidays in Kenya; German tourists would come down to the pool in the early hours of the morning and leave their belongings on the best loungers, then go back to bed. One morning, Michael, my husband in those days, became so incensed by this activity, he tipped loungers and belongings into the pool whilst the Germans were breakfasting. There was one almighty fracas!

First job is to call housekeeping to arrange some badly needed laundry service, unlock the window and report the bathroom light not working. "Madam needs to place the keycard in the receptor near the door to operate the lights, laundry will be collected, please use the bag and form provided. I will arrange for the window to be opened, thank you. Is there anything else Madam needs assistance with?". "No that's all thank you" Madam has only been here 5 minutes, there's time!!!

I feel as though I am on a different planet to the one I have been on for the last 2 weeks and whereas all these niceties are rather a treat, they are all so unnecessary. I feel distanced from reality. However, I guess that is the aim. The clientele pay to be removed from the reality of the rubbish in the river and the seedy areas like Jyaira Thamel and the little flock of bluebirds sitting in the dust. The guests here are the businesspeople from India, Pakistan and Europe who stay here to discuss the problems with Nepalese officials. They wine and dine; all go home and leave the next generation of bluebirds in the same dust.

It is only midday and rendezvous is at 4pm on the roof terrace with the group and the tour leader. There is plenty of time to go and familiarize myself with the new surroundings.

Up market coffee shops, gift shops, department stores catering for the real climbers, tour companies advertising all the well-known treks including Everest, Annapurna and Tibet. There is precious little else and I find myself walking back in the direction of Durbar Square and the area where I have spent the last 3 days.

For the first time since I left New Zealand, apart from time monitor flights, I now have to look at my watch to be at the group meeting. As usual, I am late, and the proceedings are well under way by the time I arrive on the rooftop garden and swimming pool area. The pool looks very inviting but the disapproving looks coming from the gathering, I guess for my timekeeping, dissolves that idea. I take the empty seat, am asked to introduce myself, and attempt to pickup on the talk. The women outnumber the men and all appear to be younger than me apart from one man, maybe in his sixties, quite unkempt in comparison to the others. A moon-faced Nepali, the tour leader, introduces himself as Ramesh. The most striking thing about him is the large mass of black hair protruding from his ears. I must stop looking or I am going to have an attack of the giggles! The meeting is backtracked in order that I can familiarize with the group by means of introduction to them all. Greg, Australia; Hai, originally from Vietnam, now living in Australia; and the women all from Australia, apart from my room buddy; Susan, Meryl, Karen, Tash and Saumya, originally from Sri Lanka. It comes to the older man travelling with a Nepali companion: "Names are not important; I am on a spiritual journey, not one to make friends!" With that they both leave the meeting and a surprised gathering.

I hear several unsympathetic comments before the discussion continues around the advised preparation for this trip; the fitness training for 3 months beforehand; the equipment needed *etc*. I remember the pages of notes that came with the itinerary, I did not have time to read them all let alone do any of it. Pushing a wheelbarrow laden with mulch up and down the hill at the back of my home, hundreds of times, was my fitness training, which could be classed as hill walking with a backpack! Smoking is my serious issue. I have come armed with packs of Nicorette patches and chewing gum, and ashamedly they have remained at the bottom of my case. So far, my contribution to this enthusiastic comparing of preparation is zero! Oh this is a good start!

The topic moves on rapidly to the cost of the visa needed for Tibet and the tips recommended for the cooks, drivers and porters. There is an immediate outcry of protest when Ramesh informs us the visa cost has doubled and the required amount for tips has trebled. Well, that is going to tear a hole in my budget. Tipping remains an unresolved point, and Ramesh beats a hasty retreat on the issue, which is to be decided once the journey is completed rather than at the start. I notice that everyone has a very large red holdall sporting the expedition name and logo. There is one left parked in the corner, mine presumably. I take the opportunity to cause a distraction from the heated discussion by walking over to collect it; goodness it is a weight, I hope we don't have to carry these. The distraction has worked, all are now focused on my investigation of the bag's contents and explaining the things inside.

"That is your sleeping bag, that is your down filled coat, try it on."

This was obviously for someone at least a foot taller than me, larger in girth, and with very long arms, as I disappear from view once inside it. I can hear the laughter and feel a person trying to find me. Ramesh is busy rolling the arms up, and pulling the waist cord as tight as possible to take up some of the length, which is well past my knees. As my head pops out the top, Ramesh's ears are now within 6 inches of me. I cannot contain myself any longer. Fortunately, the gathering thinks I am laughing at the coat! The mood has lifted considerably, so on that note the meeting is called to a close with the parting assurance from Ramesh, that the others will explain the sections I missed.

Back in the room, Lorraine or Rainy as she likes to be called, explains how the kit bag system works, what to take *etc*. She is a pharmacist from Mt Maunganui, an ideal partner for a smoker and one whose lifestyle, eating the right thing and so on is almost catastrophic verging on "how do I exist"!

"You sort all you are taking. Everything needs to go in the holdall; so just the essentials, the rest stays in your case. Tomorrow the case goes down for storage. Flight tickets and valuables can be left in the hotel safe, did you read the guidelines on what to bring?"

I watch all the trekking gear, most from the store "Kathmandu", a well known outward bounds stockist of all "the right equipment", that Rainy is busy putting in the bag; the well worn walking boots, modern backpack *etc*.

"I'll do mine later, think I will have a walk, see you later."

The roof and pool area are the only smoking zones within the hotel, that is where I am headed to reflect on the comparison with what I have brought for this journey and what everyone else seems to have. My walking boots still have the price tag attached, trousers and woollens from the Salvation Army charity shop. I did purchase new socks, thermals and waterproofs and my backpack, again obtained in a Charity shop, was a gift from Janet. It is the old canvas type with not too many bells and whistles, but most important it is the colour of monks' robes! I wonder if the man with no name is as prepared for this journey, or if, like me, he is more reliant on spiritual protection!

WEDNESDAY MAY 27TH

Breakfast finds everyone in an enthusiastic mood as the group is off to tour Kathmandu and Swayambunath. I am going to detach, and find Kopan monastery about 10kms out of the city. I notice the man with no name and his companion are taking breakfast in the large outside area, complete with cascading water feature, alone. Ramesh appears in buoyant mood and eager to herd everyone to the waiting bus for their tour, I make my excuses but am intrigued to know the stranger's name.

"His name is Ferris, his travelling companion is from Mustang, his name is Tenzin They would rather be left alone, that is no problem" is all Ramesh will divulge. I wonder if I can tag along, at a distance, with the rather-be-left-alone party, as it has already become clear the main group are really rather noisy Australians. I find a small table and chair outside, away

from Ferris, and bathe in the gentle sound of the water meandering over artificial rocks into a large pool, it is heaven!

"You will be advised to take a taxi to Kopan Madam, much safer for you"

The concierge is quite concerned that I am enquiring about the local bus to my destination. The cost of a taxi is significantly more than local transport, then there is a waiting fee for a fixed time, which is going to put me back on clock watching.

"I will be fine on the bus, is the bus station within walking distance?"

"15 minutes madam, I still think you would be better taking a taxi"

His concern for my safety is causing me some reservations but not enough to dissuade me from my original plans. Even with a map I am finding difficulty in navigating my way round Kathmandu, so I take a bicycle rickshaw to the central bus station. Chaos is an understatement and finding the right bus is like looking for a needle in a haystack! The system seems to be similar to the share jeep concept in Dharamsala. I later discover it is called the microbus. Each vehicle has a young boy on the roof shouting out the destination, in Nepali of course, which is of little help to me. I am totally bewildered and amazed that folk can hear the boys' shouts for customers as the numbers take the level of noise to the point where the destination is indistinguishable. The real worry is that all the ones I ask with a simple word, "Kopan", they all say "Yes" and offer to take my money! I look for someone who can help, and spot a young woman in college uniform.

"I am looking for the bus to Kopan, can you speak English"

I recognize the Tibetan features as she turns to answer.

"Yes, I speak English, please to come with me, I am also going there, come please."

We squeeze into the bus, the fare is about NZ$2.00. My new friend tries to engage in conversation, but the noise from a missing exhaust pipe makes it impossible to hear her. We head out of the city into the suburbs. I catch glimpses, through the filthy windows, of the mile after mile of half finished projects. Houses, apartment blocks, road resurfacing and construction, some of it apparently abandoned or work stopped for lunch! This is Nepal trying to modernize without the funding or expertise, a global problem, which seems to increase the poverty and misery for so many of the population. Land swallowed up by developments and swollen city numbers that are full of expectation for a future they had only dreamed of, and are still dreaming of, but now full of frustration. The gangs of idle youths are everywhere. The rubbish is still mounting with no end in sight to the strike. The newspapers continue to highlight the political wrangling for power. Nepal is in a dangerous vacuum, with the Chinese there on the doorstep waiting to capitalize on the situation, and take another step closer to India.

In 2008 during the international 10th March anniversary of the uprising of Tibetans in 1950 against the Chinese occupation of Tibet, there were graphic pictures, printed worldwide, of the Tibetan nuns that had protested peacefully, being subjected to terrible beatings by the Nepalese army—their blood and tears running together like a river as

they were thrown into the cattle trucks waiting to take them to prison where many died. This is a stark illustration of how the long standing agreement with Nepal and the safety net given to the Tibetans is in tatters under instructions from Beijing.

Suddenly the bus comes to a grinding halt. All passengers depart but my friend waits on the roadside for me and explains there is no road further on and that the walk is about 2kms to Kopan monastery. We are in a small village which is where she lives and the next thing I am invited for refreshments and an offer to come with me to the monastery, as the track is rather rough and the incline quite steep in places. I accept both offers gladly and follow her into a dilapidated apartment block up a series of broken concrete steps and into a tiny room. The only window is partially boarded over with cardboard, and the one bare light bulb hanging from a dangerous looking wire that loops its way from behind a cupboard to the ceiling. This leaves some of the room in shadow, hiding the obviously cramped living conditions. There are three camp beds, a small sink and a portable gas ring for cooking. Piles of books and papers are everywhere, as are clothes and all other sundry items necessary for living. The centerpiece is of course the television which must have its volume set at the maximum and is entertaining two children sprawling on one of the beds. The girl is frantically trying to find a place for me to sit whilst shouting at the two youngsters who get up, turn off the TV and leave the room rather reluctantly.

"I don't mean to disturb your day, it is not necessary to turn off the TV, your children were in the middle of watching something"

They are my brother and sister. There is a problem with the school, so they stay home.

Please sit here would you like some water"

I am offered the end of one of the beds and accept the water. We begin to talk, the first thing I learn is her name, Dawa Dolma, age 21 and just finished college. She has been supported by a Norwegian family although I don't think they have ever met. Her English is excellent but evidently, she has now reached a crossroads in life. Because she is still classed as a refugee she cannot find a job, and she will not be considered for Nepali citizenship until she has work. A catch 22 situation that has almost been designed, I feel, to keep the Tibetans from considering Nepal as a home. The choice is either to return to Tibet or to go South to India. I do not ask where her parents are, or how it is she has the responsibility of younger siblings, but the anxiety of the situation shows in her young face. I just want to scoop the three of them up, put them somewhere safe, give them a new start, somewhere decent to live, let them know they are wanted and loved, I want a miracle not just for Dawa Dolma but for all Tibetans who are in this and worse situations. She passes me a sheaf of papers and a glossy college magazine.

"My end of year results and teachers' appraisals, the magazine has photos of my year, let me find the right page"

She sits down beside me and flicks through the pages, my eye is caught momentarily by a short verse.

"Can you just go back a few pages, something I saw that I would like to read"

"A thing of nature
Not a cruel creature.
I don't think of the future
Just I am a good creature.
Flowers grow in me
Birds sing with me.
Animals play with me,
But humans kill me.
I give H_2O
You give CO_2.
I give you life
You take my life.
You cut my branches
To make some benches.
I have also feeling,
But you kill with no feeling.
I am the beauty of nature,
Thick and tall is my structure.
I am the protector of the future,
Save me and you will get pleasure."

I reflect for a moment on the words, and feel he is almost talking about his country, Tibet.

"How old is this boy who wrote this"

"His class year means he is about 12years maybe 13, I will cut it out for you to take"

"I don't want to spoil your magazine, but yes I would like very much to take this with me, thank you"

She goes to find scissors from the cupboard and as the door opens, a pile of paper falls out, what lands at my feet is extraordinary. An official looking booklet, torn at the edges, but open at a page that displays the face of an older man, rubber stamped, with a few faded words in Tibetan and Chinese. I pick it up and hand it to her.

"My father, not long before he died, this was his passport. He returned to Lhasa. My mother is still there I think. I don't hear anything of them anymore; it is not good to make enquiries."

Her distress is obvious and I have an attack of claustrophobia coming on, it seems an opportunity to remind her of the 2kms walk to the monastery.

"Please wait outside, I will only be a short time thank you."

I find a stool in the open corridor that overlooks the backyard. Rubbish is piled up along with a broken bike and concrete. There is a strong smell of urine—I guess the sewerage system is none to efficient.

We head out along a narrow track through small allotments. It is uphill all the way and with the time approaching midday the sun is fierce in this open landscape. Dawa has a large, heavy umbrella as shade and insists not only on giving me the greater protection, but carrying it all the way. My protests to let me share the burden are met

with the simple answer.

"You are my elder, it is not right for you to carry."

I muse that would I ever hear such a sentiment in the West!

The ground is starved of water and the small amount of crops are dying. The rains are due soon, and they need it. Dawa tells me much of this land will go for development eventually. I hope the current tenants are given a fair deal. The view is getting better the longer we walk. The air is much cleaner and it is good to be out of the city and seeing something of the Nepal I remember. I can see the top of Kopan Monastery. Not much further to go and, once again, my unfitness is beginning to tell.

Kopan is one of the first monasteries to be developed by Western Buddhists, and is one of the main centres for the development of the Mahayana tradition, the middle road between Vajrayana and Hinyana, the other two Buddhist traditions. Mahayana forms the central core of the Dalai Lama's teachings in the West. Much has been done globally to preserve the purity and clarity of this tradition.

As we approach the steps that lead to the main gate we stand aside to let a monk and a nun pass. I catch a glimpse of his face, and carry on for a couple of yards before stopping. I turn and call back:

"Excuse me! I know you. I think you came to New Zealand last year and gave teachings at the Dorje Chang in Avondale."

They turn to face me. The monk looks rather surprised, then a glimmer of recollection comes into his eyes.

"I remember saying if you were ever in Nepal to pay me a visit, and here you are. We are on our way out for the day, you found us just in time, it is nice to see you"

We chat for a while about my forthcoming trip to Tibet and he issues a warning:

"Don't believe everything you see or everything you are told, much is not as it appears to be"

Rather like the true nature of reality is what comes to my mind. We bid each other farewell. I hope he comes back to New Zealand. As we continue on our way to the main gates, I ponder on this chance meeting. Had any part of the day been just a little different I would either have missed him or not found him within the walls of the monastery where hundreds of monks reside. It would have been embarrassing and hopeless to explain that I was looking for a monk whose name I had forgotten!

We finally reach the main gates, which are well and truly closed. I look at Dawa rather despairingly but she is not concerned and gives me a big smile and rings the very large bell. We wait several minutes before a voice can be heard from the other side of the gate. Dawa responds in Tibetan, so I am lost as to what is being said, but whatever it is, it has

done the trick as one of the gates opens to admit us.

The brilliant noon light bathes the beautiful temple entrance in it's golden veil. The thousand armed Chenrezig is in the forefront of the huge stupa, housing The Buddha. The colours are brilliant and the views wonderful; the ambience bringing one into a natural meditative state. Dawa explains that the monastery is now closed but they have let us in for a short time. The temple itself is out of bounds, so we walk the khora, soaking up the smells, sounds, and tranquility.

Kopan houses approximately 300 monks with a nunnery close by. It was founded by Lama Yeshe and his student Lama Zopa Rinpoche, who is now the spiritual director, after Lama Yeshe passed away. Sadly we cannot enter the temple or stay for long, and soon find ourselves being ushered out.

Downhill all the way, we soon reach Dawa's village and the bus stop. She waits with me to ensure I get the right bus. I don't think from here they go anywhere else apart from the city. I thank her for all her time, hospitality and carrying the umbrella for the duration. She gives me her email address, at least I think it is hers, and we bid farewell as the bus arrives. I am sad to leave her, and so wish I could do more to help but it takes money and a good deal of it.

It is 4pm, I am back at the Radisson. There is no sign of Rainy, so time for some reflection on my day. The large window is open with a cool breeze causing the lace curtains to gently billow. Two weighty pigeons are perched on the window ledge, which is approximately

5 feet wide by 4 feet deep. I coo to them but they seem disinterested in conversation. The thought of going to the roof just to have a smoke seems to much effort, so I sit close to the window in order that the room will not be unbearable for my non-smoking companion. Without really thinking about what I am doing, I get out of the window onto the ledge and join the pigeons. I am four stories high, have no idea how many feet up and normally I get vertigo standing on a chair so I just don't look down! The pigeons seem rather disconcerted about being joined as they move away—seems like the whole world is anti-smoking! I hear some shouting from down below, and choose to ignore it, but as the shouts get progressively louder I have to acknowledge that they are being aimed at me.

"Who moi?" I say, pointing a finger at myself.

"Madam please return to the room."

I look down to see several of the suited management waving frantically in my direction.

"Madam s'il vous plait!"

I guess they think I might be French!

With a wave and an *au revoir* to the birds, and to the relief of the distraught figures below, I clamber back through he window just as Rainy enters the room.

"There is rather a scene downstairs; people rushing around outside, and pointing."

"I think it might have something to do with me, I sat out on the ledge with the pigeons to have a smoke."

She is quite horrified that I would do such a silly thing, and is correct in thinking that the window would be shut and locked at the first available moment.

"We are about to ascend to 5000 metres" I remind her, albeit not on a window ledge above a car park in one of Kathmandu's better hotels!"

The pigeons never came back and I have probably taken another step backward in the estimation of my traveling companion!

I have found an inexpensive Italian café not far from the hotel, where a delicious bowl of homemade soup and bread costs about NZ$3, and is a meal in itself. The rest of the group stay in the hotel and seem quite happy to pay the extortionate prices in the hotel restaurant. It is also my time for quiet reflection on the day's events and my trying to accustom myself to traveling with others, whom, apart from Ferris and Tenzin, seem to have little knowledge of where we are going, or the true reason of the trip. For most it seems to be just another challenging hike. I have yet to sort out my kit bag and find a suitable place to conceal the radio stickers, the precious pills and the items given to me by Christine back at the monastery in New Zealand, for taking to the sacred mountain, Mt Kailas.

Rainy is still up, thankfully, by the time I return to the room. Most of the gifts purchased in Dharamasala and the books that would be confiscated by the Chinese if I take them into Tibet, are already packed in the case ready for storing. Within 10 minutes I am finished. I have split the stickers into small bundles, some inside the cameras, others in my socks and concealed amongst the various medicines that I have for every complaint known to man, and which, apart from the painkillers for the bus ride back to Delhi, I have had no need for. I have started the diamox for altitude sickness with no side effects. I am unsure if Rainy is watching my rather strange packing, but I doubt if she would have me arrested!

It is 2am and I cannot sleep. The room seems small and stuffy with no fresh air and my mind is anything but still. I creep out of the room as quietly as possible, head for the lift and the roof garden. The security guard is surprised to have company, and quite happy to take a cigarette before he launches into his life history. I work at staying interested, although I would so enjoy some peace and quiet. He is evidently working at two jobs, a day one plus this night security work in order that enough money can be accumulated to send him to England to study economics. His family is helping and his goal is to go there in one year's time, and stay for 3 years. This is a huge challenge financially, for any young man and I admire his determination. It is nearly 4am by the time I get back to the room. Sitting at the window waiting for the sunrise, I watch the few early morning workers, porters, kitchen staff, cleaners and the like arrive to start their long day.

THURSDAY MAY 28TH

The mood at breakfast is one of anticipation, excitement and a few nerves combined with a flurry of activity. Suitcases are being brought down for safekeeping; passports returned from the Chinese visa department; red holdalls piled up for loading onto the coach. I flick through the pages in my passport looking for the visa for the Tibetan Autonomous Region, as the Chinese refer to Tibet. Nothing! No stamp, no visa, nothing to say that I am going to Tibet. It seems strange that I am about to cross an international border into a highly controversial part of China with no entry visa. I am disappointed that there will be no physical reference to my being in Tibet—as far as my passport goes anyway. Finally we get going. The short journey to the airport is used by Ramesh to introduce the Nepali sherpas, who make up the camping staff.

The airport is heaving with humanity and red tape. Nepalese are not renowned for their administrative skills at the best of times, let alone when there is a pandemic scare on. We have to stay as a group, so everyone has to have the correct paperwork including the exit and return visa for entry back into the country at the Friendship Bridge border between Tibet/China and Nepal. Ramesh is eager to get through to the gate waiting area, leaving no time to visit duty free. I feel as though my independence has gone.

We wait for what seems like an eternity in a large shed along with hundreds of others, mainly Indians, for the Air China flight to Lhasa to be called. Finally the call comes and we walk out onto the tarmac under heavy Chinese security. The flight is only an hour in duration and I hope, once again, for clear skies that will allow Everest to reveal her summit. The overhead screens show continuous Chinese propaganda on the area now known as Tibetan Autonomous Region, China's western cultural heritage. I cannot watch. Suddenly there is great excitement. Everyone clustered to the left of the aisle, pulling cameras out of bags—Everest. Chomolungma is her Tibetan name—Mother of Tibet, her massif brazenly piercing the clouds, the light illuminating every snow flake. It is magnificent sight—the highest point on the planet. It is hard to believe Sir Edmund Hillary once stood there with the New Zealand flag. The backdrop is the deep sapphire blue of the sky, and I feel suspended in time above her grace and beauty. The noise of people and engines fade into the distance, my tears now falling with the emotion. Being brought back to the reality of the plane, we are told to return to our seats for the descent, and as we emerge from the clouds the panorama of Tibet unfolds below me. I have tried not to pre-empt what I would see or how I would feel. Nothing has prepared me for this. I am at home after 55 years of waiting.

Entrance to Kopan

Headless Sphinx

Kathmandu Valley

Giant Dorje or Vajra

Guru Rinpoche. Swayambunath

Stupas at Swayambunath

Dawa Dulma's apartment block

Home of a Tibetan nun

Dream Gardens

Dream Gardens

At last. Tibet from the air

Mt. Everest or Chomolungma from the air

TIBET
MAY 28TH–JUNE 15TH

"Let the roar of the Snow Lion be heard across the Himalaya,
Let the thunder of his pads be felt across the Himalaya,
Let him sit at the feet of The Dalai Lama,
Let his flag fly high above The Potala."

We touch down, taxi to the terminal and wait, and wait, and wait. When the doors finally open a long stream of men in white boiler suits, shoe coverings, gloves and face masks fill the aisle. They say nothing, but gesticulate for all passengers to place a thermometer, which they are giving out, under the armpit. This is like a movie as we sit there for a good ten minutes cooking our thermometers! A record of each individual's temperature does appear to be recorded as they are collected. We have been sitting on the tarmac for a good half an hour when at last we are allowed to disembark and directed into a small but modern terminal building. Ramesh gathers all the passports and takes them to the desk along with a bundle of other papers. Then horrors of horrors, I see mine being subtracted from the rest and put to one side. There is some discussion between Ramesh and the officials but I can see by the look on his face that it has been to no avail. There is no explanation and I am told to wait with three other Westerners, apparently traveling on their own, whilst my group is directed to the other side of the hall. They are not permitted to pass through security without me. This is my first sense of the reality of the Tibetan situation. Tibetans go through this ordeal and far worse every day. Fortunately, in a way, there is divine intervention. It seems that Ferris has a slightly higher than normal temperature, the whole place seems to go on red alert as he is surrounded by men in the white boiler suits and rushed into a side room. I can see the concern on the faces of the others as we sit and wait for the outcome of Ferris's examination. The other passengers from the plane are all through security and customs and we still wait. I can see my passport still isolated from the rest although interest in it seems to have been overridden by Ferris and his temperature. After nearly an hour he emerges from the side room with the all clear. I simply walk over to join the group half expecting to be arrested or something, instead we are all hurried through security and out, with not a second glance at my passport.

At last my feet are on Tibetan earth. I had promised myself I would do prostrations at this moment, but the Chinese security are here in force and with the delay the waiting coach is under pressure from them to exit the car park. We have a Tibetan driver and a young looking guide both anxious to be away from the airport.

The road is wide and in good repair which will make the one hour journey to Lhasa fairly comfortable. We seem to be the only vehicle on the road, and the landscape is quite barren and empty. No one on the coach is saying much. We all just stare at the nothingness. Rainy is already thumbing through her Lonely Planet guide, maybe in the hope that we may come across a "suggested site to visit". I have no emotion; my mind is as blank as the landscape. As we round a bend, the coach slows and pulls into a car park already congested with other coaches and four-wheel drives. A large group of tourists are busy with their cameras taking pictures of a large carving of Shakyamuni Buddha in the facing rock. I am pleased we have stopped, I need to stretch my legs and find a quiet

place for a smoke. I will leave the tourists to do their thing. Before I have managed to find my cigarettes, the young Tibetan guide is at my side offering a taste of my first Chinese smoke: "Tho che chey, thank you"

We are already at 4,500 thousand metres above sea level, and combined with the rough tobacco I inevitably start a coughing fit. The guide is very concerned that he has maybe contributed to this and is full of apologies. I can feel my lungs searching for oxygen, and my brain telling me "you should not be doing this" and the eyes of my traveling companions saying "what idiot would carry on smoking at this altitude!" The guide rejoins the group in order to give a commentary on the carving, which is obviously quite new and probably crafted by Chinese as the work is clumsy and the colours garish. I listen in. Nothing is said about the history of it, just the subject matter and there is plenty to say on Shakyamuni. We leave the area with the group in a more positive mood, now we have seen something to confirm we are in the land of the Buddhas.

The next tourist site is a cluster of newly built Tibetan style houses, literally parked on the side of the road. We slow but do not stop. The slower speed enables me to see down one of the dividing alleys revealing the squalor behind the pristine front façade. I notice the Chinese red flag aloft on every roof. Well above the height of the few prayer flags. The young guide is sitting in the seat ahead of mine. He has the aquiline features of Eastern Tibet, either Kham or Amdo, closely cropped hair and, I would say, in his late twenties or early thirties.

"What part of Tibet are you from?" I enquire. He seems shaken by my question, but

answers in good English,

"Central part" is all the reply.

I probe a little further until he finally reveals he is not permitted to refer to any part of Tibet using the Tibetan geographical names. It is time to change the subject as I can see quite clearly how nervous he has become by what must seem my inappropriate line of questioning. We have not yet arrived in Lhasa, and already the tragedy of Tibet is apparent.

As we approach the city outskirts, the organised mind of the Chinese is visible in the tree planting scheme. Hundreds of straight lines with not much sign of food crops. Barley is the staple diet of Tibetans, which when ground and mixed with water becomes *tsampa*. When Chairman Mao and the Red army invaded Tibet in the fifties, all barley was replaced with wheat. The obvious consequence was tens of thousands died of starvation after the crop failed. This area was once one of the main growing regions but as we approach Lhasa the skyline is a sea of concrete. The mood on the bus has taken another slide, which deepens as we now enter Lhasa along a giant causeway. Hundreds of large Chinese lanterns line the route; massive office and apartment blocks, all glass and concrete, are flanked with wide pavements and huge advertising billboards. It is bright, garish, and sickening. The tears tumble uncontrollably down my face. I knew this was going to be a difficult time trying to remain detached emotionally. I have almost been dreading what I would truly find here, and after only a couple of hours the reality has hit home hard. There is total silence from the others until Susan breaks it with:

"This is China, not Tibet"

Ramesh is on his feet urging us all to look left; we are approaching the Potala. I finally have in my sights the building that I have only ever dreamed of seeing. This magnificent architectural achievement of mankind is now dwarfed by Chinese construction, looking slightly lost and forlorn, but none the less still there. Tall iron railings surround the perimeter, as well as a large number of army personnel.

We arrive at the Hotel Himalaya with its wide, pillared overly ornate entrance typical of just about every building I have seen so far. Room allocations are made and we are instructed to meet in the foyer at 4pm for a tour of the Barkhor and the famous Jokhang Temple. Always my first job from any hotel room is to check the view. Absolute horror, I am looking straight down into an army barracks and parade ground, complete with the afternoon drill and a Chinese rendition of the Australian song Waltzing Matilda! This is unreal but it has me laughing it seems so ridiculous. Rainy is a very organized lady, having done various treks before and is soon out of the room in order to be at the rendezvous in plenty of time. Having the space to myself gives me time for reflection and the concealment of the radio stickers *etc* that I am taking with me this afternoon. The windows open without the help of housekeeping, so I watch the finish of the military drill whilst trying to accustom myself to the harsh Chinese cigarettes. The skyline is not completely obscured by buildings. I can see the rich brown tops of the mountains, bare of snow, but cast under this oppressive red shadow of China.

I am the last one to rejoin the group. Everyone looks well prepared with walking boots, day pack *etc*. The temperature is surprisingly warm, and I am still in the white leather sandals that I have worn continuously since India. I know there have been a few giggles about my bizarre footwear, but they are very well made and comfortable. Ferris is in shorts which has also raised a few eyebrows. We board the coach and only travel about 5 minutes before we arrive at the Barkhor and all disembark. Being the religious month of Saga Dawa, the streets are bustling with pilgrims completing the Khora around the perimeter of the Jokhang Temple which is positioned at the centre of the Barkhor, a public square. For the first time since our arrival I feel there is something of Tibet remaining. It lifts my heart and spirit and I release all the condemnation and anger for China into the wind, and follow the singing of the hundreds of prayer wheels that are carried by all that surround me. It is as though I have stepped through a door and am able now to take hold of the underlying strength of the Tibetan people, that continues to resist the brutality of the Chinese occupation. As I walk with the pilgrims this strength is getting deeper, coursing through every fibre of my body. I know I am home. The question of why my passion about this country, its people and the Dalai Lama has taken such a hold on me over the years is being answered at last. And so begins a reunion that I never dreamt or imagined could happen.

The Jokhang Temple, alongside The Potala, are the most revered buildings in all of Tibet. The Barkhor was once a calculated series of narrow lanes forming the outer circle of a Mandala on which the whole area was fashioned. A Mandala is the power circle of the Buddha, used for meditation. It is either depicted in a painted way or made from

sand. It is the universe, holding all precious things, and its centre is most powerful. The following history of the Jokhang is taken from a booklet published by Tibet House and The Tibetan Museum I visited in Dharamsala. Amazingly the publication is sponsored by the Duchess of York, Sarah Ferguson.

Tsuglag Khang, the Tibetan name for the Jokhang, or Central Cathedral, is the most sacred temple in Tibet. It was established in the capital in the seventh century by King Songsten Gampo to house the image of Akshobhya Buddha offered to him by his Nepalese queen, Trisun. At the time it was called Rasa Trulnang temple. Only later, when the Jowo Shakyamuni statue, given to the King by Wengcheng, his Chinese consort, was moved here from the Ramoche Temple was it given its present name, Jokhang, or Shrine of The Jowo. The Jowo statue was originally given to Wengcneng's father, T'ai-tsung, the second Tang emperor, by a King from Bengal. The Tibetans believe it was crafted by the celestial artist, Vishvakarman at the time of the Shakyamuni Buddha. When Wengcheng made the long journey to Tibet she was accompanied by many Chinese artisans who built Ramoche to house this statue. The Jokhang was originally designed by Nepalese craftsmen on behalf of Queen Trisun.

I have lost sight of the group, thank goodness, and make my way to the entrance, past the large dome-shaped structures that burn juniper. It is believed that to place juniper twigs on the flames and watch the smoke go skyward from the narrow opening at the top, is sending ones prayers to the deities. It is a meritorious action and the aroma from the burning leaves is wonderful. I join a handful of Tibetans completing their prostrations to do likewise. A long queue has formed within the barriers waiting for their turn to enter the Temple. I cannot see many police, but I am sure there are plenty of plainclothes personnel and surveillance cameras. Without thinking, I slip into the middle of the queue, without consequence and without causing any disturbance amongst those I have joined. Their bodies seem to close around me as we wait our turn. My head is slightly bowed so as to not catch the eye of anyone who may think to question my being there. I wonder if my silver hair is going to attract attention, amidst the carpet of normal black! We shuffle forward, I start to lose track of time as we enter a dark, covered passageway where I feel less conspicuous. Now seems the perfect time to distribute the precious things that I have concealed. Fumbling in the dark, with heart beating I open the little silk bag and start with the coloured threads, keeping my hands low, and indicating with eye contact to those nearest me that I have something for them. Within seconds I am mobbed for the entire contents. Outstretched hands appear from nowhere, the nervous tension is tangible. As we move forward toward the end of the passage and the light, I cast a quick glance trying to calculate how much time we have to complete the job in hand. Time is running out so the last of the pills I give to those nearest me, gesticulating they should be more fairly handed round in a less precarious situation. People are touching my head, holding my hand, touching my arm. I can see the big smiles as the gloom lifts. I feel almost crippled by the emotion of the last few minutes, so privileged to be here and give out a tiny ray of light and hope—the message from His Holiness that his people are not forgotten or forsaken.

I am cocooned in Tibetans as we start the journey through the Jokhang, a maze of small shrines each housing a deity. The Green Tara, Guru Rinpoche, Tsongkapa and his disciples are some of those we pass. Offerings of money are placed at every one, money the Tibetans can ill afford and is taken by the Chinese, but it is still offered nevertheless. I smell the scent of the hundreds of butter lamps, intermingling with juniper and incense.

Most of the time I keep my head down, I feel invisible as long as I do not engage eye contact with those I know are here and who know I shouldn't be. Suddenly a nun appears from nowhere. I see her wizened features, her small stature, feel her hand clasp mine. Her other hand rests on my head as she begins a prayer or blessing. Her eyes hold all there is to know about embarking on a spiritual journey, and they lead me in, if only for a brief moment. She is gone as silently as she arrived. I am guided through the throng and catch a glimpse of the Jowo Buddha before being almost catapulted by my escorts into an outer part where the barricades stand in force alongside dozens of large prayer wheels. I look back, the faces have changed, I have no idea where exactly I am but following the barricades finally leads me back to the front of the Jokhang.

I see Ramesh frantically waving at me

"You must stay with the group" he is shouting.

I have no reply, my mind is in another place. I am brought back to the others who seem unsure of why they are here or what to do.

"You are not permitted to enter The Jokhang today, there are too many pilgrims, no tourists" is the speech delivered by Ramesh.

"We will meet here in one hour and go for dinner, so please to look around, do not get lost."

He heads off in the direction of the coach that delivered us. The group forms into smaller groups and begins their self-guided tour of the Barkhor. I am amused to see them all going in the same direction, but separately! This leaves Ferris, his Nepalese companion, Tenzin, and myself. On the clockwise route, or Khora, around the Jokhang is a mass of small stalls selling all the Buddhist and Tibetan paraphernalia one could imagine. The carefully designed route has been destroyed and replaced with wide open spaces, so typical of the Chinese. This has allowed large troop movement during the many clampdowns and mass arrests that periodically take place. The visual passage from the Barkhor to the Potala has now been blocked by a huge dump of earth with the intention, I presume, of cutting the link between the two. The Tibetan stallholders are desperate for any business with pleas to look at their wares. I concentrate on the hundreds of people that we have joined, most in Western clothes, but the odd one or two in traditional dress that depicts the area of Tibet from which they have come. Many wear hats pulled firmly down over their eyes and do not want to engage in eye contact. Mala beads are being counted, the hand prayer wheels spun and the prayers are being quietly spoken. There is a festival air, appropriate as we are celebrating *Saga Dawa*, the period in which Buddha was born, found enlightenment, and gave his first teaching at Sarnath. Ferris seems to be buying something from every stall, and soon has an armful of mala beads. A small silver gau, or locket, catches my eye and with some bargaining is my first purchase in the city of Lhasa.

The hour is soon over as we make our way back to the meeting point, pick up with the rest of the group who are all suitably sporting their purchases and follow Ramesh. The first two restaurants are full, so it is third time lucky. As we approach the entrance I am beginning to feel inexplicably uncomfortable, and hang back. The proprietor sees everyone in but as I meet the doorway it is though I have walked into a wall. Perspiration is running in rivers, I have a thumping headache instantly pounding through my skull and am completely unable to follow. Ferris and Tenzin notice and come back

"I can't go in here." I have panic in my voice.

I can see a large room, empty of guests apart from us and, of all things, a huge stuffed bear.

Ramesh comes back

"I'm sorry I can't stay here, I have to go somewhere else."

There is annoyance on his face. Ferris takes him to one side, comes back.

"It is OK, we will go to another restaurant with you, come on let's go"

We go back to the first restaurant, and find that it is full as they are hosting a wedding reception. However the owner disappears for a few moments, comes back with the news that we may join the other guests. After congratulating the happy couple, an American groom and a Tibetan bride, and thanking them for allowing us to join the reception, we have a thoroughly enjoyable evening.

The room is in darkness by the time I get back, and realize it is going to be difficult to write my notes regularly unless I use the public areas of the hotel. It is hard sitting amongst the Chinese décor, Chinese staff and seeing glimpses of Tibet portrayed as tourist souvenirs, whilst trying to document the fact that the heart has been torn from this land and the people left isolated and afraid. My first day in Tibet will be embedded in my mind for eternity. It is a day of tears accompanied by some extraordinary events and ending with the joyous occasion of a wedding signifying a new start for one Tibetan girl and the freedom of America.

FRIDAY. MAY 29TH

As the itinerary for the day is relayed to us over breakfast, I am already planning on how many times I might get conveniently lost! We now have the young Tibetan guide with us and the first stop is The Potala. The Chinese have been very thorough in stamping their mark on everything including the elaborate entry ticket now needed to enter the abandoned home of The Dalai Lama. As we begin the ascent up the wide stone steps, the magnificence and the reality overwhelm me. I am truly walking the steps that so many great Buddhist masters have done before. The altitude is really telling on my breathing and I fall someway behind the others. The Tibetan guide comes back and I finally learn

his name—Tashi. Once inside the outer perimeter three sets of wooden stairs, the left for going up, the right for descending and the centre closed off, as these would have been exclusively for His Holiness, take us up into history.

The Potala Palace symbolizes Tibet and means "the Pure Land" which is a joyful and pure state of mind, as opposed to an actual place. It is a landmark that used to be seen for miles. Little remains of the original 11 storey Palace which King Songtsen Gampo began building on Mount Marpori in 637. Construction of the present Palace began in 1645, during the time of the 5th Dalai Lama. By 1648 the White Palace, or Podrang Karpo, was completed. A team of 7,000 workers and 1500 artisans were employed on this massive project. The Red Palace, or Podrang Marpo, was added, between 1690-93, by the regent Desi Sangye Gyatso. He concealed the death of the 5th Dalai Lama so that the building could be finished without the political upheaval which would follow such an event. In 1922 the 13th Dalai Lama restored many of the chapels and assembly halls in the White Palace and added two stories to the Red Palace. The current Palace contains 1,000 rooms and covers 130,000 square metres. I feel like an intruder—a trespasser. This place and its power were for those who had the learning to understand the depth of the Buddha's teachings; eons of reincarnated Dalai Lamas and Rinpoches. Although it has been totally abused and is no more than a grandiose tourist attraction with only a few rooms open to the public, I have great respect for its past, and all that it represents. There are hordes of Chinese tour groups, their leaders using hand held megaphones to relay distorted historical facts, effectively drowning out any other guides.

We have only been given 30 minute to complete the tour and, strictly, no cameras are allowed. The Dalai Lama's throne is one of the few things I remember clearly; the rest is just a rushed walk through a maze of corridors. I keep falling behind, to the irritation of Ramesh, in order to try and get my bearings, but things have been moved, or missing, it is a jumble of artifacts put together in the public areas with no cohesion. We emerge onto one of the roof tops, the view is stunning. Suddenly plainclothes security are everywhere. An Indian tourist has managed to smuggle a pocket camera in and within seconds of him taking his first shot, the camera is confiscated and he and his group are being removed. I look out across Lhasa Valley, once called the 'Lung of Lhasa', now just a concrete mass. True to the pictures I have seen the giant monolith, a celebration of Chairman Mao, stands right in front, centred in a vast paved concourse that has no meaning or purpose other than for military movement. To the right is the children's theme park I have heard about and a boating pond complete with garish paddle boats sporting heads of cartoon characters, fairground rides and candy floss sellers. To the left the Chinese have built the main Government offices and police headquarters. These are the symbols the Chinese use to celebrate their "liberation of Tibet and its people" and a constant reminder to Tibetans that their beloved Potala can be easily overshadowed and to defy the Party line is dangerous and useless. Even though I have never seen any photos of the interior, I have had some vivid, terrible dreams about what has gone on in this place; I care not to recall them. Our 30 minutes is soon passed and I join Ferris and Tenzin on the walk back to the carpark. We say nothing.

The next location is Dreprung monastery, some 15 minutes drive from the city. This was the largest monastery in Tibet before 1959, when it was almost raised to the ground by the Chinese People's Liberation Army. It was built in 1436 and was the most important centre of political power in Tibet's early history. When Tibet turned to Buddhism, over 70% of the male population became monks with Dreprung housing one of the largest monastic populations of approximately 10,000. On the walk up the hill to what is left I ask Tashi how many monks remain, and am shocked by his answer. "About 200."

The street sellers are out in force waving their prayer wheels and mala beads in the hope of a sale. Ferris goes into action yet again. 'Whatever is he going to do with all these purchases?' I muse to myself. We are permitted to take cameras into Drepung for an extortionate fee, but once again we are rushed around what is left of the interior. The wall paintings are scarred and faded, parts have been undergoing restoration but the colours are garish and incorrect. The images of Shakyamuni are here along with various deities, the identities of whom I am not sure. It is all beginning to be rather confusing, the whole day conducted at pace with limited introduction or dialogue from Ramesh or Tashi. As I am always someway behind the group I generally miss anything that is being said. Rather I choose to feel where I am, to touch the dimly lit statues, run my fingers along the walls and across the paintings that have seen it all. I silently offer prayers and leave the token gesture of a few cents. I will not leave more to the Chinese. We go out onto one of the rooftops; the concrete jungle spreads out again across the valley. There is some sort of ceremony going on, 3 suited Chinese officials shaking the hand of what I must assume be one of the Drepung Lamas. The Chinese flag flies aloft in the background, behind which is a large pile of rubble. I manage to stray a little off the beaten track on the way out, taking pictures of the damage that is still evident. This time it is Tashi who reels me in and we are off to the once huge kitchens that fed 10,000 monks. The light is very poor but I can see the giant cauldrons and ladles stacked in tiers almost to the ceiling. There is one elderly monk, taking the money for camera use, I immediately pay him. I have yet to really master this large camera so hope for the best.

There is a wall effectively cutting this hall in half, or so I feel, and the more my eyes adjust to the darkness the more I know this place. The monk is watching me as my gaze travels along the high shelves and back to the cauldrons. There is an earthen floor, which holds me still while the others leave quite unimpressed. This time I see Ramesh waiting patiently outside in the late afternoon sun. With a small bow to the monk, whose eyes seem to penetrate my every thought, and a "*tho che chey*" (thank you), I join the others for the walk back. As I run my hands over the outer walls it is though I have had an electric shock. I am covered in goose bumps the size of Chomolungma herself! I suddenly feel tremendous elation, almost happiness and now have a smile from ear to ear. The others have gone on ahead so I just stand here absorbing this wonderful; feeling. I pull a piece of lichen from between the cracks and push it into my pocket. Now I know that this place is more than familiar to me. I don't want to leave, but Tashi appears from round the corner, waits for a moment so I know I have to go. It is a real wrench against the pull I feel to stay.

I try to talk to Tashi on the way back to the coach about what truly is going on here, he

looks into my eyes,

"We cannot speak here, wait until we have left the city, then we will talk. We are old friends."

He knows what I have been experiencing since my feet stepped onto Tibetan earth, another re-affirmation that this is not my mind playing tricks, or a delusionary desire. It is real. On the way back to the hotel Tashi walks down the coach and asks me to give him the silver *gau* that I am now wearing around my neck. I look at him quizzically, say nothing and hand it to him. He answers my question without words.

That night we all have dinner in the Lhasa Kitchen restaurant. One or two are experiencing Delhi belly and other altitude symptoms, including Ferris who is now on a diet of potato soup only. We walk back to the hotel through the backstreets and I see the seedy side of Lhasa night life. There are reportedly some 200 brothels here to cater for the Chinese soldiers. We walk through the Moslem sector, witnessing some late night halal butchery. Again that overwhelming sadness follows me like a shadow and I cannot detach from it no matter how hard I try.

Writing my notes on the day's events, I recall all the moments, since I left New Zealand, that can only be put down to causes and conditions, or Karma. Even before I left, certain aspects of the planning seemed to follow the same path. I came upon this trip by accident when I thought I was contacting a UK-based travel company, only to discover they have offices in Auckland. My enquiry was just to "go to Tibet". My place was the last one remaining so the booking was complete within an hour. I had no preconceived intention of embarking on a 48 km walk at over 6,000 metres. The second hand camera was the result of bidding on 5 previous Trade Me auctions, without success. In frustration the 6th attempt I hit the pay now button. When I collected it from Devonport I found the young man had been taken to Tibet when he was 3 years old, by his Buddhist mother. Slowly my path here has been opening, as a chrysalis finding her wings in that single moment of rebirth.

SATURDAY MAY 30TH

This is the last day here in Lhasa before we embark on the 1200kms drive across western Tibet to Mt Kailash. Norbulingka, or the Summer Palace, is our first stop. It is reported that some 30,000 Tibetans surrounded Norbulingka in March 1959 to protect His Holiness the Dalai Lama from arrest by the Chinese Army. The following night he, his family and others left Tibet on the long trek to India and safety. Tashi leans over from his seat in front and returns my *gau*.

"What is placed inside is for your protection."

All I can see is a minute piece on monastic robe, protruding from the clasp.

We enter what was once the beautiful garden to find much of it overgrown and in decay.

The entrance courtyard is now adorned with brightly coloured pots and plants, many of them, I discover, are plastic. Again we have little time, but I am surprised to feel how homely it once was by the remnants that remain. The Chinese groups are emphasising recognition of the flush toilet in the bathroom, as if to point out that His Holiness is a mere mortal, not a God. We are limited to what we are allowed to see once again, but the little we are allowed to see gives me the understanding of why His Holiness much preferred to be here, rather than at The Potala.

Outside there are Tibetans picnicking in the grounds, a favourite pastime in local culture. The most upsetting part of this visit is to see that open ground toilets, with old plastic as a screen, have been allowed not far from the building. They are a stinking mess and an obvious attempt to deface the name Dalai Lama. There is no way that any of us are going to use them. It is during this hunt for alternative toilet services that I find I have lost the group. I return to the summer palace in the hope that I may be admitted again. An old monk is standing sentry in front of closed doors. I give him an appealing look, he opens the doors for a moment in order that I can glimpse the golden Buddha that sits just inside, but that is all. I read the sadness in his face, and again that sense of recognition which brings us both to a large smile.

I meander through the grounds with a sense of relief being away from Ramesh and the group. Then I spot my first cat! A small black sitting in the long grass, amber eyes that follow my approach, letting me know that she is ready to move if I get too close. I keep my distance and watch her move off through the long grass. It is nice to see a few local families enjoying their picnic, children running around, some laughter and smiles. To date I have seen very few children—toddlers and babies, yes, but older ones, no. I come across a small shop selling "genuine artifacts", more like Chinese replicas than anything genuine. I find the entrance and am now aware of how much time has passed. There is no sign of the group, and I am being carefully watched by Chinese security guards who monitor the visitors entering. I smile politely and return to the grounds. I know I am going to be in trouble with Ramesh as I return once again to the entrance gates. This time I see him coming toward me, almost at a run, he is not a happy man! I do not receive the expected reprimand, just a reminder that by becoming detached from the group, I am placing the rest under threat of the tour being cancelled by the Chinese, and sending us back to Nepal.

We are now on our way to Sera Monastery, to attend the 3pm debating session. This is the third of the great Gelug monastic universities. Founded in 1419 by one of Tsongkhapa's disciples, Jamchen Choeje Shakya Yeshi, the great Assembly Hall, 3 colleges and 30 residential units, housing 6,000 monks were decimated by the Chinese. Now there appears to be no more than 50 or so monks, and the small courtyard hosting the debate is a far cry from what was once a huge and noisy affair. Debating is an important part of Buddhist practice whereby a junior monk and his senior will argue a point, the senior clapping his hands with great gusto when he feels he has won the argument. It tests the individual on his knowledge and understanding in all areas of Buddhist philosophy and conduct. There are more tourists here than monks, busy filming on cameras of all descriptions what they see as a true representation of living a monastic life. I see it as no more than a small stage show, and find a quiet corner

to meditate, in the hope of hearing echoes from the past.

Back at the hotel the group book themselves in for the "Tibetan night" a buffet followed by a floor show of Tibetan dancing performed by TIPA, Tibetan Institute of Performing Arts. I look at the large billboard advertising this extravaganza, knowing full well that the members of TIPA were arrested and detained in 2008 during the large scale demonstrations. The heavily painted faces look almost ghoulish and it is impossible to say if they are Chinese or Tibetan performers. I, like Ferris and Tenzin, decline the group night out! I return to the Barkhor on foot, Ferris and Tenzin have gone off on their own. It is 5pm and the stallholders are beginning to pack up. I purchase 5 khatas, one to take to Kailash, the others to take back to New Zealand. There is one stall selling monastic attire and, with some bargaining, purchase an outer woollen robe for Lama Pasang. It is going to be difficult to carry to many large or heavy items all the way back to Nepal. I take this opportunity to place the last of the radio stickers in the fruit and vegetable market which seems to be the beginning of the older Tibetan quarter. The alleys are narrow and many of the houses have crumbled away or are in the process. There are no tourists here and no police, at least not in evidence. I come across a recently demolished home. The locals are retrieving whatever building materials they can, but it has left the neighbouring building precariously unstable. An older couple, sitting on what is left, wave to me. I return the gesture. They keep waving, and the woman calls out across the chasm that was once a home.

"You must leave here, it is not safe for you. Go! Go!"

Stunned by her comments I move quickly to find a way out of this maze of alleys, which must have been part of the Mandala accessing the Jokhang. The concentration of police tells me I am heading in the right direction, as they start to cordon off the entrances to this part of town. I now realize there must be a curfew restricting the movement of Tibetans after 6pm. I find the restaurant where Ferris, Tenzin and I had supper, this is a better place to reflect on the day and write up notes. It is my last night on this whirlwind tour of Lhasa—such a mix of sadness and happiness. It is better not to attach to either emotion, just allow space for each, and join together in the natural law from which they are formed. I have not really seen Lhasa, only a contrived snapshot, edited with tension, surveillance and fear. The most obvious sign of repression is that I have not seen one monk apart from the few in the monasteries. So tomorrow we move on across western Tibet, with the hope that Tashi finds his silenced voice.

SUNDAY MAY 31ST

Today is the first of many early starts; breakfast and packing all done by 7.30am. We are now assigned to places in 3 Land Cruisers, all with Tibetan drivers. Rainy and I are paired up with Ferris and Tenzin, I notice a sigh of relief coming from the others that they do not have he pleasure of Ferris's company. Poor man he continues to aggravate some and his delhi belly has not subsided. Tashi is also our guide, I think by request, and introduces us to our tall driver, I think he is from Kham.

"I am Gaga" comes the booming voice, followed by a wide smile displaying a set of well worn teeth. He is rangy in stature, and wears an assortment of western give-aways, some of which fits! I notice he carries an old well traveled yak skin saddle bag, more in keeping with a man from Kham. The red hold-alls are piled into the back of the two big support trucks that carry all the camping gear, food, petrol *etc*. Ramesh is in his element giving orders and we are quickly on our way. Being the smallest I get the middle of the back seat, consequently with the two seat structure firmly between my buttocks and the back of it set between my shoulder blades. Well Rainy can have a turn here is all I can think to myself.

We have only been going for about half an hour when clouds of steam erupt from the radiator and the convoy comes to a halt. We wait for nearly an hour whilst deliberations are held as to the remedy needed, before we start to investigate our surroundings. I go up to the top of a rocky outcrop and find a small lake at the bottom. A few locals are gathered with three large black bags, busy emptying the contents into the water. I join them to see hundreds of fish fry being let loose, a gesture that is seen to bring good fortune and happiness. The lakes here are now being netted by the Chinese, all but destroying the existing aquatic life. As I make my way back, to my astonishment and amusement, I see the rest of the group are in the middle of a yoga class, conducted by Saumya.

Our destination is Gyantse, 3,977 meters above sea level, for an overnight hotel stop, and a tour of the famous Tashi Gomang or Kubum monastery with its great octagonal Stupa. Finally we are on our way once again. The road surface is good, fortunately for the radiator header tank, which has been fixed with the aid of a wire coat hanger. We are descending down the Kyichu Valley to the Yarlung Tsangpo, or Brahmaputra river, before ascending up Khamba La, or Khamba Pass at 4,900 metres. The scenery is breathtaking. The sky clear blue, so much so that we are almost upon the Yamdrok So, or Turquoise Lake, before we realise it. This vast expanse of freshwater, covering 754 square kilometres, is one of the most Sacred Lakes in all Tibet. We stop for photos. Tashi and I take a short stroll and he tells me that the Chinese have built a hydro electric dam here to service the ever growing needs of Lhasa. This is seen as further mutilation of a Sacred site. Several more stops are needed en route to cater for Ferris's prolonged stomach trouble, and we pass through two check points. We are heavily scrutinized by Chinese guards and the passports are meticulously gone through from cover to cover. It is a long wait.

We finally roll into town, and what a sad sight. Construction seems to be everywhere; the air is thick with cement dust being blown from the piles of discarded building rubble. The hotel has the typical grandiose frontage, but the rooms and public areas are tawdry and neglected. Rainy, in customary fashion, is well organized and ready for the rendezvous within 5 minutes. I am left in my usual chaotic muddle and the welcome moments on my own. The hotel rules list the fines payable for breakages, right down to the light bulbs and also, in bold type, state that the manager's permission will be required if guests wish to dress in Tibetan attire. This I must photograph!

We walk to Kubum; the terraced exterior has 108 gates, 9 levels and 75 chapels. Within the chapels, the images form a progressive hierarchy of three dimensional mandalas, ensuring that the Stupa encapsulates within it the entire spiritual path. The wrathful

deities are on the lower levels and the more peaceful on higher tiers. It is beautiful, even though so much of it is neglected. Once again the areas that have been touched up are in bright garish colours—completely wrong. Situated to the right of the Stupa is the Monastery. For the first time since we arrived in Tibet we may be able to witness a prayer ceremony which is in progress. Tashi has a quick look and nods that we can go in. One or two tourists are already here, standing along the back wall, watching. Our group join them, no photos are allowed. Tashi takes my arm, and takes me over to one of the long benches that seat the monks. There is a space and I am invited to sit and join them. I have never seen the style of hat before; tall red crowns with a series of flaps extending to the shoulder. Under the flaps is what looks to be false, long black hair. A *puja* is meditation which is chanted or sung, and I make a guess that this is what I am now a temporary participant of. I cannot understand the words, but no matter, the experience itself is enough as if my mind were being bathed in a subtle rain of transmission. I am brought back to reality with a tap on my shoulder. Tashi is waiting, time to go. There are no words to describe these few minutes here.

I think the religious sites are beginning to be rather monotonous for some. Street sellers are in abundance and we descend on one that is selling a CD of the monks chanting, "A Prayer for Peace"—I live in hope. Above the monastery is the Dzong or Fortress; most of which has been rebuilt and, I believe, now houses an anti-British museum!

We are left to explore the town with two hours before the rendezvous for dinner at a local restaurant. Most of the group stays together, I go in the opposite direction. There seems to be only two main roads. All the shops are Chinese, newly built, and most with loudspeakers attached to the frontage, blaring out Chinese music and presumably encouragement to enter and buy. I notice all the Chinese pedestrians walk on the pavement whilst the Tibetans are forced to walk in the gutter. The cars are all driven by Chinese, with one or two locals in horse-drawn carts. The police station is not hard to find, being the largest building in town, and that seems to be it, not much at all. The dust is terrible and most people wear face masks, hiding the very tangible sense of despair that permeates this town. I don't want to return to the hotel any earlier than necessary—just for a quick shower and a change of clothes. As I keep walking the same two streets I am aware of a black four wheel drive that has been a short distance behind me for some time. I do a 180 degree turn; sure enough the wagon is behind me again. A quick glance backward and I see the windows are blacked out, hiding the occupants. I don't feel fear, but that anger has returned—'OK so you want a chase do you?' It is too dangerous to leave any of the radio stickers, which had been my intention, as I go into every shop that is open. The wagon parks each time, and eventually we arrive back at the hotel, I give a wave goodbye as I finally see them drive off.

There is chaos in our room and I find a distraught Rainy.

I'm glad to see you" is her frantic greeting. "Take a look in the bathroom."

What a mess, half the ceiling has come down.

"Whatever did you do?" I am laughing. "No chance of a shower now."

"I am going to find Ramesh." she is not finding this funny, and is gone.

I look in the book of rules for the fine payable if one brings the ceiling down!!!

MONDAY JUNE 1ST

Another early start to the day and no mention of the bathroom ceiling from the hotel manager. We are off to Shigatse, the seat of the Panchen Lama, the second highest figure in Tibet. Situated at 3,840 metres above sea level, Shigatse is the second largest city in Tibet. Poor Ferris is now plagued with a bladder infection as well as the ongoing bowel problems. As a result we stop every 10 minutes or so, which gives me the opportunity to relieve my butt and back from the middle place. Rainy is reluctant to swap, as she, like some of the others is finding Ferris increasingly intolerable. He is rather abrupt at times, and reluctant to divulge much about himself. Every night he and Tenzin take themselves off on their own, so really we don't see that much of him. Tashi and I share a smoke during these stops. Nothing is said, unless Gaga joins us. He likes to chat and cuddle! Sadly on the next stop Karen, travelling in one of the other vehicles, comments on Gaga's embraces. I take Gaga to one side and have to ask him to curtail his behaviour as something improper has been suggested. He is horrified and I am saddened that even up here people bring their oh so typical misconceptions with them.

The route takes us through what was once the fertile valley of Yarlung created by the

Yarlung Tsangpo and Kyichu rivers. Now it is no more than a wasteland, mile upon mile of building rubble and general rubbish has been left to contaminate the green plains of the past. It is reminiscent of the coal mine slag heaps in the North of England. We catch glimpses of the river periodically which, at a guess, is only 30% of its original width and volume. There are one or two settlements way in the distance, with small herds of sheep and yak grazing on very little. However to witness this ever decreasing sight is both sad and precious. Nomads have been systematically rounded up, their lands confiscated along with their animals. Large resettlement programmes have been in force whereby they are dumped in their thousands into concrete housing blocks miles from anywhere with nothing. I have seen pictures of such places and they are too similar to prison camps to be called anything else. I ask Tashi why all the settlements display the Chinese flag. His answer:

"They are forced to do this."

Gaga is a seasoned driver. We make the 140 kms journey in good time, even with the multitude of stops needed for Ferris. We arrive by lunch time, and find a much larger town than Gyantse. The hotel is of better standard but still typical Chinese style. I notice in the lobby there are shops selling Tibetan artifacts and mannequins dressed in Tibetan regional costume. All are clearly labeled "Tibetan cultural relic". We are not given long before the statutory group tour of the famous monastery, the Tashi Lhunpo, begins. The name Tashi Lhunpo means "all fortune and happiness gathered here", and certainly the air is much more festive and buoyant than in Gyantse.

We start with lunch. I watch Ramesh as he tucks away yet another full Nepali platter, enough for four people—a once if not twice daily occurrence! I manage to drop a few of the radio stickers in the tips box along with 5 yuan. We walk to our destination, and queue to pass through the recently installed iron security gates into the huge open paved concourse. Much of the original, now crumbling, buildings are on my left, most cordoned off. The renovated part, encompassing the entrance with a large overhead bell and the three flights of steps, are to my right. It is a delight to see so many Tibetans here, especially the children. I stop to take photos of two women picnicking on a grassy slope that borders the many steps taking us to the tourist part. With beaming smiles I am invited to join them and although I cannot understand much of what is said, it is an unimportant detail which we soon overcome by using that which is beyond speech. I find Tashi waiting for me and we enter the place that has seen the abduction of the true, current Panchen Lama and the murder of his predecessor.

The monastery was founded in 1447 by Gendun Drub, the first Dalai Lama and Je Tsongkhapa's youngest disciple. It is one of four great Gelug tradition monasteries and has always been the seat of the Panchen Lama. The small part, which has been renovated with heavy Chinese influence, is in readiness for the proposed residency of the Chinese appointed Panchen Lama. After they abducted the true reincarnation and his family, the Chinese Government was quick to fill the void with the son of one of their high officials. His photograph is everywhere, whereas all photographs of the Dalai Lama have been removed here and at all the other sites we have visited. It is a criminal offence to have any picture of His Holiness, both for Tibetans and tourists. Punishment is a mandatory prison sentence of 10 years. The one experience I have truly been looking forward to is seeing the giant statue of Jampa Chenmo, or the Maitreya Buddha. It stands at over 26 metres high and contains 279 kilograms of gold and 150,000 kilograms of copper and brass. The hands are in the symbolic teaching *mudra*, and he sits in European style. A new, modern interpretation of Maitreya is currently under construction in Kushingar, India, and will be the largest statue on the planet when completed. I gaze upward to meet the face of the future Buddha and am lost in its beauty, and power. All around me is absorbed into this union that is unfolding; the pull of energy and calm, the two in unison, a guiding light into a flawless mind. I am being pushed and jostled by the hundreds that wish to stand in my place, how many millions of eyes have met with those of Maitreya and how many more will have the fortune of doing so before either the Chinese tear him down in fear, or his time of coming ends the human suffering that prevails in the present. It is customary to leave a small piece of ones clothing or similar. I remove the plaited wristband that I was given by one of the stallholders outside the Namgyal Temple in Dharamshala. I tuck it behind a *khata* fixed to one of the ornate pillars on my right. There is a narrow passage way that circumviates the statue. There is very little light, but I can feel the earth floor has a furrow worn into it from the thousands of feet that have paid homage here. The brilliance of the afternoon light in a cloudless sky, showers us as we emerge from the building to continue our tour of the remaining complex. The epitome of the Chinese domination here is in the form of the dreaded tourist souvenir shop. I pass it by while the others gather to buy their mementos. Finding myself on my own again, I set out into the areas that have been cordoned off, and take as many photos as possible before I find Tashi behind me with a worried look. Instead of returning to the tourist zone, he guides

me down a narrow track toward a small shack.

"There is someone here I want you to meet."

A small goat greets us at the broken gate, the only entry point in a stone wall, constructed out of what I assume to be the stone from the destroyed, greater part of the original monastery. The home itself is almost indistinguishable from the ruins that surround it, and the face of the old nun that emerges bears the same hallmark of senseless destruction and brutality. She only just gets to the gate when we have Chinese security bearing down on us. I have time to clasp her hand and slip some money into it before we are escorted away. I can feel Tashi's nervous tension as we are greeted by Ramesh's disapproving look. Tashi is immediately summoned, I assume for severe reprimand. There is nothing I can do to help.

Once out of the Monastery we are left to make our own way back to the hotel. This time Rainy comes with me. We pass endless street souvenir stalls, which are now the only means left to the Tibetans to generate any kind of income. It is heartbreaking to have them pleading for us to buy just one thing. In a short time I accumulate various bracelets, some *katas*, a *vajra*, the Sanskrit word for dorje, or Sacred Sceptre. This is the thunderbolt, the indestructible power of truth cutting through delusion. It is always accompanied by the bell, the five pronged handle of which, represents the axis of the universe and the four directions. We stop at a piece of waste ground which is being used as a picnic area and watch, with admiration, the few families carrying on the tradition as best they can.

Dinner is in a local restaurant. I nearly part with too much money for a beautiful painting of nomadic horseman, which is hanging on the wall. This is our last night in a bed for tomorrow we start the long drive to Kailash, and will sleep under canvas. It is also the last night I am able to sit in relative comfort to write up my notes for the day. I find a piece of writing, a description of the Tashi Lhunpo, from a Captain Samuel Turner, a British Army Officer, serving in the Embassy to the Court of Teshu Lama in 1783.

"If the magnificence of the place were to be increased by an external cause, none could more superbly have adorned its numerous gilded canopies and turrets, than the rising sun in full splendour directly opposite. It presented a view wonderfully brilliant, the effect was little short of magic, and it made an impression which no time will ever efface from my mind."

My own conclusion, in the form of verse, that condenses my feelings on what I have witnessed these last few days are more subdued, but offer a sort of prayer in the hope that one day Captain Turner's words reflect the future, rather than the past.

"Take the gilded light of truth supreme
To fight the shadow, living unseen.
Grasp hold the Buddha's throne in pure lapis blue
A radiance like no other.
Let it flow as rain on the demon within,
See the rainbow colours born of wisdom and emptiness fill the vajra cup.
Drink this nectar, its course to transform
This withering flower into new bud
And bloom once more."

These words were originally inspired by the serious illness of Saumya, some months after my return to New Zealand, and with whom I have stayed in close contact since our trip. With one or two alterations I find them equally applicable to this part of my journal.

TUESDAY JUNE 2ND

Please buy everything you need here, and take enough money, there is nowhere for either these things once we have left" are the instructions from Ramesh as we finish breakfast. Several requests to find an ATM cash machine and a general store for the chocolate addicts and those needing extra toilet rolls are submitted. Rainy goes through a check list with me and I suddenly have a shopping list! Sunglasses, lip balm, water, woollen hat are top of my growing list.

"That will do." I plead, as I can see my budget being left in tatters as well as having to carry all these things. The one item I have been looking for is a yak wool sweater or jacket. The shopping takes longer than Ramesh planned, but we all find what we need. My brightly coloured, thick woollen hat with ear flaps is a good buy, and I can't resist a bottle of water labeled "Tibetan Magic Water".

Within 10 minutes of starting out, the road disappears into rough terrain. Gaga's speed slows slightly, and after every large pothole or boulder shouts "Sorry, sorry, sorry" as bums leave seats, shoulders crash into the side of the vehicle, and heads hit the roof. Ferris is beside himself with anger at Gaga's lack of sympathy with his ongoing bowel and bladder issues and demands an immediate toilet stop. We have traveled all of 20 kilometres, and my feelings are:

"This is going to be a long and arduous journey."

We begin to fall a long way back from the rest of the convoy. The Himalayas, in the distance, take us along their course. Their grandeur distracts from the abysmal foreground, one of polluted, barren grasslands. We pick our way through intermittent road excavation works, blasting of rock, and shoring up the many landslips that have occurred due to poor materials used in the attempt to carve a road from Shigatse to Kailash. Most of the work force is Tibetan, both men and women, working with little more than buckets, shovels and wooden carts. They clearly live on site, judging by the makeshift shelters which are no more than tarpaulins, forming small communities on the side of the road. It is a bleak existence.

We arrive at the first checkpoint about two hours from Shigatse to find that one of the other guides from the third Land Cruiser has made a huge blunder. Tashi leans through the open window to explain.

"She has left all the paperwork in the hotel at Shigatse, they are not allowed to continue without it."

It is decided to leave the passengers at the checkpoint, whilst the driver and guide return

to the hotel, a round trip of 4 hours at best. We, and the second Land Cruiser, along with the two support trucks, are to continue and establish the campsite before darkness falls, as it is already nearly midday, and we have not covered half the estimated 450 kms drive.

Tashi looks back from his front passenger seat: "This could cost her the job."

Things don't get any better. We have to stop not just for Ferris, but a reoccurrence of the faulty cooling system. The non existent road becomes a sea of mud, the support trucks are finding it difficult to stay upright, and not get stuck. The situation really goes downhill when the second Land Cruiser sustains both a puncture and a rear shock absorber failure. Tashi and Gaga take off for the nearest settlement in the hope of finding some spare parts. Unbelievably the vehicles only carry a sparse toolkit and not much in the way of spares. The wait on the roadside seems to go on forever when they finally return with a replacement tyre but nothing else. We have to continue with the useless shock absorber, poor Susan has the seat directly over the side that is now delivering bone crushing jolts at every bump. It is just past midnight when we limp into the campsite. The temperature has dropped. No one is speaking. A hot meal is ready for us, accompanied by gallons of black tea. I stagger out of the mess tent to find Rainy, it is pitch black and very, very cold.

"Jane, in here," I see her head pop out of the flap, "don't trip over the guy ropes" My head is splitting with the mother of headaches as I try, with the aid of a torch, to figure how the sleeping bag works. We are shoulder to shoulder in a tiny nylon bubble, the large kit bags take up valuable room. Fully clothed I manage to get into the sleeping bag, and as my head hits the ground, the headache turns into an Everest avalanche. Claustrophobia sets in, as I now struggle to extract myself from this straight jacket and out of the bubble. Rainy says nothing. I don't know if she is asleep, she can have the tent to herself, as I manage to scramble out into the cold. I return to the deserted mess tent where I spend the following five hours on the verge of tears, but with the comfort of being able to smoke a cigarette without the scrutiny of my fellow travellers and Ramesh.

WEDNESDAY JUNE 3RD

The sunrise sees most of the group tired and dispirited. The vehicle that was left at the checkpoint, we find out, arrived about 2am. I didn't hear them. The echoes of the headache are dealt with—thank heavens for Nurofen! Ramesh assures me this is altitude sickness, so I increase the Diamox tablets, and plan not to complain too much as there is a risk that I will be taken back to Shigatse. Breakfast is a hearty affair with porridge, eggs, toast and the standard black tea. I have my own coffee and milk powder as both are non existent here. The disabled Land Cruiser has been taken to the nearest village for repairs, so we have time to absorb our surroundings and take it easy. The tour company's notes describe our first campsite as being in a sheltered spot on yak herders' pastures, close to the Tsangpo river but in reality we are camped on the side of the road amongst the excavations. The wind has whipped up a dust, so everything is grey. There is water nearby, just a trickle and a bridge crosses it just beyond our camp. It is adorned with hundreds of prayer flags, a reminder that we are in Tibet.

Saumya soon lifts the mood with another session of yoga. I join in, a complete beginner, and continue the moves without extinguishing my cigarette. This causes great hilarity and I discover that on one of the later sessions they all pretend to be smoking, taking puffs of an imaginary smoke during the passes of the arms, which became known as the "Jane Move". The vehicles are back by 10am, the camp has already been dismantled and we are on our way. The snow clad peaks on the horizon rise and fall and the landscape becomes more spectacular. We ascend two passes bringing us to a height of approximately 6,000 metres above sea level. At the top of each pass the thousands of prayer flags release their mantras to the heavens. The one thing I have been waiting for, and am now standing in the midst of, is the noise. The high wind stretches their lines taut, the flimsy material dancing in a kaleidoscope of colour against the backdrop of the snow covered mountains. The sound explodes in my ears, and the tears again fall. My few flags join the others as I offer prayers for the release of Tibet, and all the suffering of mankind. We pass small herds of sheep and yak, the occasional herd of wild ass, then there is great excitement as three white-lipped gazelles are spotted. These have been hunted by the Chinese almost to extinction. The convoy stops in order that photos can be taken, and just to admire their beauty and elegance. Mile after mile of barbed wire reign in the natural landscape, with one or two clusters of dwellings in the far distance. Tenzin sits in the front with Tashi and they chatter on in Tibetan. Ferris, despite his intestinal problems seems unusually light hearted. He engages me in conversation on the scenery, asking me to take photos for him from the truck, through the open passenger window.

We stop for a packed lunch, and all try to find a suitable rock or mound to screen the call of nature. Rainy has suitably nicknamed this necessity as a "marmot stop". It is amusing to see a row of heads peering from behind boulders—like meercats. We camp on the roadside again, not very picturesque, but the river, albeit no more than a stream in places, is our source of water. The afternoon wind whips up the dust and hurls anything not lashed down into oblivion. Dinner is amazing, considering the circumstances. A three course meal, in Nepali style, as the camp crew are all experienced Nepalese sherpas. Everyone is in bed by 9pm. I return to the mess tent to write up my notes, I am dreading the sleeping bag. It is absolutely freezing, with a gale force wind ballooning inside the tent. I am trying out the headlight, loaned to me, but every time I look down to write, the thing slips down onto my nose. I try to hold the pen without removing the snow gloves, impossible! I break into a fit of the giggles, which in turn lead to violent hiccoughs. I recall the romantic image, portrayed to me by the owner of the headlight, of how I would be sitting under the stars, moon illuminating the mountain snow, deep in meditation. No such thing! I am frozen, tired and in need of a coffee. I can't see, I can't write and have a very sore butt! I stumble my way back to the tent, hoping I find the correct one. I decide to sleep in as many clothes as possible, on top of the sleeping bag with my head at the open end in order to try and quash the claustrophobia. I try desperately not to disturb Rainy, as I toss and turn, sit up, lie down, put on the woolly hat, take it off as my ears are itchy and hot, then the headache hits with no mercy. I think from outside our tent must be rocking, poor Rainy, what can I say to her in the morning? Only apologise.

THURSDAY JUNE 4TH

"Black tea, washing water" Juddha's head appears at the entrance to the tent. I am fearful of consciousness, anticipating the thump of a headache. I open one eye in expectation of reaching for the Nurofen. No headache, so it is safe to open both eyes! I see Juddha's moon face within centimeters of mine. It is 7am. Time I changed my sandals, which I have still been wearing much to everyone's amusement, for the big walking boots.

Rainy, have you any scissors, I need to cut the label off."

"Have you not worn those yet." Her reply accompanies the scissors. "You should have worn them in for 3 months before you really need them." She stares in disbelief as I struggle with the laces.

"I'll be fine." I assure her, with some doubt running through my mind.

Breakfast over and the camp dismantled, we head off, our destination Lake Manarasarovar, or Mapham Youtso. It is only 62 kms from Mount Kailash and is 4,558 metres above sea level. Lake Manarasarovar is recognised as being the highest freshwater lake in the world, with a surface area of 320 square kms, and a depth of 90 metres. Being a holy lake it attracts pilgrims from India, Tibet and now the West, to express their devotion either by immersing oneself three times, or by a circumambulation, i.e. a *Khora*. The landscape is changing dramatically as we begin to experience the heart of the Ngari region. Mile upon mile of arid desert, as far as the eye can see; giant sand dunes, some so close you could touch them. There is nothing just a vast expanse of emptiness. The contrast of the snow capped mountains still on the horizon creates a rather surreal feeling.

"Plenty of marmot stops here." I remark to Rainy.

The occasional dwelling can be seen far in the distance. Small flocks of sheep and the odd yak graze on the sparse scrub that is trying to survive the onslaught of desertification. We stop numerous times for Ferris, his condition is slowly improving, but it is an opportunity to all get out to stretch legs. I always join Tashi and Gaga, we share a smoke between us. I love it here. I feel relaxed, the altitude nor the Chinese cigarettes no longer bother me, and Tashi is certainly more at ease.

"Is Gaga short for another name?" I ask him.

Tashi replies: "It is Gaba, not Gaga. Gaba means man from Kham."

That makes more sense. Gaba explains he has a wife, children and grandchildren. They are still in his home village in Kham, but as that area has been particularly targeted with Chinese repression, he intends to get them all to Lhasa after this trip. Tashi also talks about his wife, a nurse in the Lhasa hospital, who is expecting their first child in August. He is 34 years old, just two years older than my son Daniel. I am beginning to feel the warmth from this man, as if he were my brother or son. He will not engage on any subject if it leans toward the political situation.

We stop in a small settlement for lunch, which comprises of an egg, some cheese, and crackers in a paper bag. The crew disappears into a dwelling for a more substantial meal. I leave the group for a chance to explore and meet some of the villagers, maybe. Rotting rubbish is piled up, along with hundreds of empty beer bottles and tyres, attracting one of two scavenging dogs. They are in a sorry state, with mange and severe eye infections. These are Tibetan Mastiffs, commonly used as guard dogs, and are one of the three breeds synonymous with Tibet, the others being the Lhasa Apso and Tibetan spaniel. The most distressing sight is of small children begging. They too are in a sorry state, obviously suffering from malnutrition, and with similar eye infections. One little boy approaches me with more determination than the others. I see on his face a look of anger and resentment as I give him 5 Yuan. There is no thanks, just his back, as he returns to the wasteland along with his friends. The call goes out to resume our journey. I am quiet and thoughtful. Tashi gives me a concerned look which I return with a silent "It's OK". So very little difference between the existence of the dog and the child; a scenario repeated millions of times globally.

The landscape continues in the same vein for the rest of the journey, and we reach Lake Manasarovar mid afternoon. In the distance towers our primary objective, Mount Kailash or Gankar Tesi. We have to pay to enter the tourist scenic zone, as the Chinese now call Manasarovar, and receive another elaborate entry ticket. Our camp is established about 100 metres from the water, and we have the remainder of the day, until dinner, to please ourselves. The sky is fairly clear of cloud—blue meets blue on the horizon. I have Kailash to my right and the most stunning trio of peaks to my left. I have no idea which peaks they are so call them Kailash's guardians. As I walk I am drawn more to the tallest of this threesome than Kailash itself. The sheer mass, so close, has a magnetism that I cannot define. The water is cold. I have to summon the determination to at least put my head in three times. I don't think I can extend to a full body submersion! I stand in the water up to my knees, plunge my head in three times, and pray that this act will be enough. Oblivious to the cold, but aware that the late afternoon wind is starting up and the sun is beginning to set, it is time to go back. My feet are numb and resemble blue prunes, thank heaven for thick socks and big boots The girls have been busy doing their smalls, which are now pegged to the guy ropes. It is quite amusing coming over the crest of a small sand dune to see everyone's knickers decorating our orange igloos.

Dinner is, once again, an amazing affair, this time with the addition of a birthday cake for Karen. The biting wind and a big drop in temperature soon sees everyone heading back to the warmth of their sleeping bags. I stay to write up my notes with the intention of somehow sleeping here. I don't suffer the claustrophobia in a larger tent, but it is a lot colder. The moon is nearly full and in another two days we will see the raising of the new prayer flag pole at the foot of Kailash. This will celebrate the full moon and give rise to good fortune and happiness.

Despite the wind I walk some way toward the lake. The cold is biting at my face but it is worth the effort. The surface of the water is illuminated both by the moon and the towering snowy peaks that surround it; a shimmering expanse of natural beauty, one of the many sites that have given rise to the magical and mysterious history of this Land. It is almost possible to hear the lyrics of Milarepa, traveling on the wind, in soprano, rising

above the peaks and dropping an octave into the valleys, summoning the deities who prevent hail and storms, and those to who encourage prosperity and good harvest. To hear the roar of the Snow Lion and the wing beat of the great Garuda; to know that in the many mountain caves the great teachers, Atisha, Tsongkapa, Marpa, Padasambhava, meditated for years in solitude on the meaning of the self, of wisdom and compassion and the power of the mind. Freeing conscious thought from the encumbrances of our narrow preconceptions, and freeing us, for the short time that each of us has in this body, from the suffering of such things as anger, greed, pride and so on. It is easy, standing here absorbed in the illumination, to have a greater understanding; it becomes as clear as the water itself. The realisation that I still do have a vulnerable human body is a wake up call to either return to camp and drink the contents of my hot water bottle waiting in the sleeping bag, or die on the spot of exposure!

FRIDAY JUNE 5TH

Why is it that as soon as I think I have finally found some sleep, Juddha's head is peering into the tent with "Black tea, washing water, morning, black tea, washing water"? Without my usual caution, I open both eyes and find the deity, Manjushri, is piercing the side of my head with his sword. Blinded by the pain and unable to find my medicine bag, Rainy has gone for help. A concerned Ramesh appears with strong pain relief and some guidance. Nausea sets in as soon as I try to sit up, this, I am told, is full-on altitude sickness. I have to make a huge effort to quash any idea they may have of not allowing me to continue, so appear in the mess tent bright and smiling within 15 minutes. Today is to be a rest day, no driving, thank goodness! Apart from the relief for aching bodies, it will allow time to adjust to the ever increasing altitude.

After breakfast, Saumya engages everyone in another yoga session. I sit it out, but am amused to hear her tell Tenzin to "clench your buttocks" She clearly doesn't know that he is a well respected Amchi doctor. Amchi is the ancient practice of Tibetan medicine, which he has combined with being the Abbot of a Buddhist monastery and children's home in Mustang, a remote part of West Nepal, once part of Tibet. He has grown his hair a little and wears western clothes for this journey so as not to draw the attention of the Chinese. Ferris seems to have been also inspired to divulge more about himself as we drew nearer to the Mountain. He claims to have a close association with the Shaolin monks and be well practiced in spiritual healing. I don't know that I am convinced with either, but it is good that he is being more social. Susan, we have all decided, has a secret stash of gin! She is in real estate back in Australia, and like all focused people in that business, has brought her laptop with her, in order to keep in touch with things back home! We have privately nicknamed her Patsy, after the Patsy in *Absolutely Fabulous*, brilliantly portrayed by Joanna Lumley. As soon as camp is established, she can be seen trekking off to find a good receiving position, or maybe just to have another shot! Karen, Tash and Hai all seem to know one another from home or, maybe, other trips. Meryl is quiet, and in the same age group as myself, all the others being a lot younger. Saumya is also a solo traveler. I can't help but notice the Chanel sunglasses and quality gear leading me to think she is a

woman of substance. The lady always has a smile and a sense of humour, as well as being masterful with her ragtag yoga participants. She has ended up with a tent of her own, and even when offered, Rainy has declined bunking in with her, an offer put, I think, to give the poor girl some peace from me, and the trials I am having with sleeping.

Ramesh calls order and informs us we are to take a three kilometre walk along the lake to the only small monastery here. It is another bright day, quite warm, with no wind. The headache has departed, the lake looks glorious and the pace brisk to say the least. Soon I am well behind the others, no matter, I enjoy the solitude. One thing I have certainly discovered is that I am not the happy camper group sort, finding to much chatter rather a distraction. On one of my occasional rest stops something catches my eye amongst some rubbish lying at the waters edge. I find a hat from, I think, the Kham region. It is tatty, but doesn't seem too dirty, so on my head it goes. When I finally catch up with the others the new headgear causes much hilarity. The monastery is tiny and according to Tashi, recently built, despite the visible deterioration. The original, housing 60 monks, was destroyed. Now no monks are allowed here. Tashi always talks quietly when ever we are discussing what has happened in the various locations. Although we are in such an isolated place, he still talks in a whisper. There is a sense of hopelessness beginning to show in the cracks of his guard that he lets down when we are alone.

On the return walk we are joined, at a distance, by two black necked cranes. They stand about 3 feet tall, have magnificent black plumes for tail feathers, and are sadly under threat from hunting It is a real treat to have these in our sights.

Back at camp, Gaba is very amused by my hat until he discovers it's origin.

"No, no, take off, no good!"

"It looks ok to me, we will do a photograph, then I will give it to the lake."

The way he handles it, as he takes it away for disposal, one would think I had been wearing a dead dog!

Dinner is accompanied by plenty of chatter about hiking gear in anticipation of the challenge that is now only a day away. This is when I excuse myself for a quiet smoke and reflection on the journey ahead. I am greeted by the most amazing sunset. The giant crimson orb is disappearing into the lake, it's rays piercing the surface of the water which, in return, is reflecting shards of colour up into the mountains. My body combines with all the five elements now present, fire, water, wind, earth and space. We are as one.

SATURDAY JUNE 6TH

My socks and knickers, which I had begun to wash late the previous day and had forgotten about, are a solid block of ice in the bowl. I will let them go the same way as the hat! Breakfast is a lively affair and we are soon on our way to Kailash. It is not far, about 60 kilometres and we soon realize why Ramesh was keen to be away early. A long queue of

traffic waits to go through the checkpoint and the official entry to yet another Tourist Scenic Zone. Finally, after about an hour, we are through.

We arrive in the town of Darchen around 11am, where we have two hours to do as we please. This is the hub for arranging yaks and ponies. I see various tour leaders vigorously negotiating with the sherpas and yak owners. This is my last chance to see if I can find the illusive yak sweater, no luck up to now. The town is rather like the last stop before nothing—from a Wild West film. Predominately Tibetan, the makeshift stores, some under plastic or canvas and others more substantial, line the one road. Previous trekkers' castoffs are one component in a jumble of all types of sundry items for those who have forgotten any of the all important bits and pieces. I negotiate the rubble and rubbish along one of the side alleys, and stop at a tent that has been pitched in a rather precarious place. I am drawn to the face of a young woman inside. Her hair is coiffured in traditional braids interwoven with coloured wool. She has some beautiful turquoise necklaces and bracelets. Her earrings are held in place using the tradition of a second piece of turquoise attached to a length of string, which is looped back over the top of the ear to form a counterbalance. I am going to buy some bracelets for special friends, as this is the last chance before the *khora*. I will wear them so they have some significance, other than just being a bracelet. The woman gives me a big smile, but says nothing. She does not even try to sell me anything, just waits. I purchase three and as she gives me my change she also pushes into my hand a small embossed brass disc. I don't know what to say. Thank you seems so inadequate for a gesture of this nature from a person who has so little. It was obviously important to her that she give it. Outside I turn it over. It has the seed syllable

OM engraved on the back. I have no idea as to the meaning of the characters embossed in a circular pattern on the front. I will ask Tashi, he will know. Next door is another enterprising trader selling blankets and other assorted woollen items. There is no one attending, so I go in for a look. At the back there is a large pile of jackets and hats. There it is finally, my yak sweater. It is sleeveless, extremely heavy and the underside is a mass of huge loops in roughly spun wool. It is a bit big but no matter. I look up and down the alley for the owner, so go back to the woman who gave me the disc. She too is nowhere to be seen. Time is getting on, so I make the decision to leave what I think is a fair price for the sweater. I tuck US$30 into the place where the sweater was found, just out of view from any inquisitive onlooker.

Progress has been made with the hiring of yaks and porters, as by the time I get back to the trucks, we are ready to leave for Tarboche. Two women, from the second group that have been following us, have decided to stay in a lodge here, rather than attempt the long walk. It seems that neither are in good health. Twenty minutes from Darchen we reach the pinnacle of a long ridge. Down in the valley is a totally unexpected sight. There are dozens of tents, mostly of the igloo type, but some more elaborate. The whole place resembles, and has the feel, of a holiday camp! Our site is already established in what appears to be the western tourist area, as opposed to the Indian area. The Indians are the ones with the more elaborate facilities, including a portable toilet. As we unload our gear I realize I am going to have problems finding the right tent. I have had difficulty with six being the same! Amidst the general noise I suddenly pick up the sound of Tibet, the long horn. It drifts through the camp weaving its way on the breeze. For a moment I

am not sure if it is my imagination but no, I can hear it. A sound that I thought I would never hear again. It is only a five minute walk, over a low ridge, to find the origin. This is Tarboche, 4800 metres, the site of the new prayer flag pole. The old flags forming a large pile ready for burning. The colour, the sounds, the smell of burning juniper, to use the words of Captain Turner, a spectacle that will never be effaced from my memory. I want to be as much a part of this as possible. Pilgrims are walking the *khora* around an area that has been roped off. There are many different regions represented judging from the different style of clothes. Wild-looking, tall nomadic people in fur trimmed hats intermingle with women in brightly coloured chubas, their heads and faces almost completely obscured by a face mask and headdress formed from a piece of yak or maybe sheep skin with an array of seashell belts around their waists, bracelets, necklaces and earrings of turquoise, coral, and lapis. One of them clutches the hand of a small boy dressed in army combat fatigues, with an ornate traditional amulet around his waist. It makes a confusing image. They are creating quite a lot of attention with the tourists and the cameras. On a rough estimation it looks like around 200 or so Tibetans are here, probably a very poor number in relation to past times. Of course the sadness is here in the form of riot control police and armoured trucks. Plastic tape and barbed wire has been used to cordon off what they deem "no go areas". They are hard to pinpoint at first, but then I see a group of twelve monks, each with a traditional instrument. The large cymbals, or *rol mo*, form the rhythm and structural outline for the chants; the double headed drum or *Nga* provide the beat; and my favourite, the long horn or *Dungchen*, is used to call the population together on important festival days. The shorter horn, which I believe to be a *Gyaling*, or Tibetan *shawm*, echoes the sounds of the mountains. Above all these sounds is the unmistakable call of the conch shell. As I get closer I realise, from their attire, the monks are from the Kagyu lineage. The Karmapa is of course the head of this tradition, and it is his portrait that I carry in the form of a small photo around my neck. I join the procession that is following the monks as they make their way to a small hut just outside the 'no go' zone. The music continues which gives me a chance to work the camera. Being small I am able to duck down and weave myself between the lower half of well built, tall and stubborn tourists. They are not allowing me an inch of space in order to get closer. By the time I emerge from their legs I am in the front row. In the past this gathering of monastics would have been measured in their hundreds, and been accompanied by traditional Cham dancers. The *Saga Dawa Duchen* is the most important festival in the Tibetan calendar, celebrating the birth, nirvana, or enlightenment, and parinirvana or death of the mortal body, of Buddha. It is held on the first full moon of the 4th month, in the Tibetan calendar, which is different from our own. It is said that all virtuous actions accomplished during this month are multiplied one thousand times. All Tibetans refrain from eating meat—it is a misconception that Tibetans are vegetarian. Alms are given freely to those in need, and new prayer flags are given the air they need to release their mantras. The monks finish their music and go inside the hut. The procession of people form a disorganized queue, with plenty of pushing and shoving. Tibetans have become notorious for ensuring their rightful place, at the front. Those that go into the hut, emerge carrying a *torma*, a gift from the monks. *Tormas* are ritual cake offerings, made from barley flour and yak butter. These are just plain in colour and conical in shape, whereas the more elaborate ones used as altar offerings are a work of art. I present a *khata* to the Abbot, as I collect mine, and head back to the camp. It seems that today's

preliminaries are over, to allow for the customary feasting and *chhang*—home brewed beer—drinking to get underway.

We have a new camp guest, a souvenir trader, who can see the potential income from such a gathering of 'rich tourists'. She has a wide beaming smile, almost filling her face, and a good sales pitch. I take to her instantly. She has an interesting amulet, made of yak skin, with a heavily embossed brass front. Set in the centre is apiece of turquoise. Of age unknown, it is well used. After some bartering I pay 50 yuan, approximately US$10. I have to laugh, as half an hour later I find her in Susan's tent with a replica!

We have received instructions from Ramesh to combine the essential items into one of the hold-alls. The other is to remain with the support trucks until the completion of the *khora*. As I am wearing all but a second pair of socks and a spare pair of trousers, I give most of the bag space to Rainy. The boots, despite Rainy's disbelief and my apprehension, are wearing well, not even a sore toe. The big down-filled coat has been a life saver at night, as has the yak sweater I have been wearing continuously since its purchase.

Tonight is the full moon. The pole raising ceremony will have been started under its brilliance, and continues for about 8 hours. Sadly the Chinese do not allow the traditional sequence of events so the pole will be put in place tomorrow morning. I retreat to the deserted mess tent as has become my ritual to write up the notes of the day's events. Without any forward planning or intention, but spurred on by the fact that I have a few of the *mani* pills left after their dispersal in the Jokhang, I decide to visit the monks in their hut. The moon offers all the light I need to scramble up the ridge toward the site. It is bitterly cold with a stiff wind. My face is numb even with some protection offered by the woollen hat pulled firmly down. The shale is slipping under my feet and clattering away behind me. The noise it makes seems deafening in the stillness of the crisp night, and the mountains echo my every move. Chinese army patrols will be maintaining their vigilance to prevent any trouble makers. Momentarily I lose my way, and as I come round a large boulder am shocked to see a group of soldiers with torches almost in front of me. Ducking down behind the rock, heart pounding, I know there will be serious repercussions if I am caught. Luck is on my side, as the soldiers finish their cigarettes and disperse into the night. I can now see the stone hut, and the glimmer of candlelight in a small window. The last 50 metres is on the flat, so the ground is more stable. I don't bother to knock on the wooden door, which is covered internally by a heavy curtain. The monks are naturally quite startled by my unannounced visit as much as by my appearance. I don't need to explain the contents of the small bag once they are revealed, other than to whisper the words "Dalai Lama", and I see them being distributed as I beat a hasty retreat. I almost run back to camp, loose my footing on the decline from the ridge and end up sliding on my bottom all the way down. With boots full of stones and a sore butt, now begins the fun of finding the right tent. Wretched guy ropes seem to be everywhere, like serpents emerging from he ground determined to snare my legs.

"Rainy, are you in there?" I call in a whisper at each tent.

"Where have you been?" finally comes an answer.

"You don't want to know."

"What happened to you, you look like you fell down a mountain?"

"It's rather a long story. You will only get cross if I tell you, best to leave it, goodnight!"

SUNDAY JUNE 7TH

A beautiful clear sky heralds this auspicious day. The campsite is dismantled as soon as breakfast is finished and the loading of the yaks begins. There are ponies and yaks everywhere; it resembles organized chaos. They are huge animals weighing 1,000 kilos or more. I watch with amusement some of the young boys trying to get these stubborn animals to do as they are told. This is the last we will see of the trucks and Land Cruisers for the next 3 days.

Following the steady procession of people over the ridge for the ceremony due to start at 10 a.m., we have been told to rendezvous at midday in order to start the days projected 15 km walk. The festival site is packed; where did all these Tibetans suddenly come from? The old flags have already been cremated, and the new pole is in place ready to be pulled vertical. Walking through the crowd, I try to capture it all on the video feature of my camera. The atmosphere is electric. Friends greeting one another; women setting up ready for their picnic; trucks being brought into position to start the lift; all accompanied by plenty of laughter and smiles. Hundreds of prayer flags and *khata*'s are being attached to the supporting ropes. People are queuing to throw their juniper offerings into the burners. The whole place is saturated with prayers for Tibet and all mankind, with such overwhelming generosity. Even some of the soldiers are taking photos and seem more relaxed. I bump into the lovely lady with the wide smile who sold me the amulet. She gives me a bear hug of an embrace, unusual for Tibetans. Her eyes alight on the small picture of the Karmapa, just visible above the layers of my clothing. I can read what she wants straight away, and within a second of me pressing it into her rough hand, it is gone, buried in the folds of her *chuba*, and her heavy coat. The Abbot takes his place in charge of the positioning of the pole. It is essential that it be absolutely straight and true, as this will ensure good fortune for the country during the forthcoming year. The horns, drum and cymbals start up alongside a truck engine and Kailash waits. She is magnificent, her snow-capped peak hand in hand with the heavens, mortal subjects at her base, now ready to heave and pull on the ropes. It all happens very quickly, with great jubilation and plenty of cheering the pole goes up. The barley flour throwing commences along with the release of the windhorses, forming an explosion of mantras ascending to the heavens. The crowd moves forward to attach more *khata*'s and prayer flags while I find a sunny spot up on the rise and watch. The presence of the mountain is overwhelming and I reflect on her importance relative to this moment and the next three days. Her Tibetan name is Gang Rinpoche, or Gangkar Tesi, and for Tibetans she is "the precious jewel of the snows" and the naval of the universe. In Bon tradition, which predates Buddhism in Tibet, she is the Swastika Mountain, the seat of all spiritual power. Indeed the shape of the swastika is very visible on her south face. Hindus trek here and pay homage to the apparition of Lord Shiva sitting in perpetual meditation. The *khora* is walked in a clockwise direction, although the Jains and the Bons walk in an anticlockwise. No one has been allowed to

challenge her summit, standing at 6,638 metres and it is said that if she ever loses all her snow it will mark the end of humanity. In 1936, the climber Herbert Tichy asked the local Gampon if she were climbable.

The Gampon answered "Only a man free from sin could climb her."

This is the most spiritual place I have ever been to. There are stories of pilgrims coming here to die, especially those of the Hindu faith. Evidently a cremation site is somewhere up there for those ending this life and entering another. My dreams and reflections are interrupted by Ferris and Tenzin:

"We have all been looking for you, it is well past 12, most have already left." It seems such a shame to go whilst all the festivities continue, but I have no choice. We find Tashi and Lakpa waiting for us, and leap into the unknown.

The terrain is not too bad at the start. No huge boulders and only a slight incline. Within the first hour the day pack has become like a cumbersome animal that I cannot shake off. Ferris has all the correct equipment, but needs frequent stops. Tenzin carries both packs, he is doing a good job taking care of the old man. Tashi is never far from my side, and if I lag a long way behind, he comes back and takes over my day pack. Westerners and Tibetans alike seem to be flying past me. Quite often families will overtake, the women carrying the youngest children on their backs, the older ones walking. One of the most incredible things I notice is their footwear which amounts to nothing more than old canvas Chinese army plimsolls. They are able to complete the entire 48 kilometres in one day, with a stop for lunch at the top of the Dolma pass!

At the end of the first 2 hours I am nearly on my knees. The walk has changed to more of a climb, negotiating large boulders and leaving the oxygen supply behind. I have started a hacking cough, the air is so thin it is painful trying to take in what little there is. My legs are like lead weights and the drop in temperature has led me to wearing the big down coat, adding to my body weight. Tashi has taken the backpack full time. I have been without him for a while, and have no idea where he or any of the others are. I count my steps; I can't even make the twenty between rests as Ramesh advised. Being so focused on the job at hand little attention is given to my surroundings or the spectacular scenery that I can only momentarily glimpse.

"Are you OK?" I hear Ramesh call. I haven't the energy to answer, and he comes to my side. We sit for a while on a rock, and he and Tashi are my aides for the next two hours or so. Apart from the help I now have, Tashi also points out the large dome outcrop, known as Padasambhavas Tomb. Further on, high above us, is the tiny monastery of Dri Puk.

We crawl into the campsite as the sun is setting. I see Ferris in front of me, in an equally dire condition. Rainy is suddenly at my side and between the three of them I am almost carried to the tent. Not once on this journey so far, have I ever been so glad to see the orange igloo. As night rolls in I think I must drift in and out of semi consciousness. Much of the activity that is going on around me is a blur. I hear Rainy and Ramesh calling me from a great distance, when I open my eyes they are right in front of me. I have been put into the sleeping bag and have 3 hot water bottles.

"Jane you must eat this. Try to sit up."

A plate of stew is put into my hand. I have hardly the energy to eat it. Next thing, Rainy is busy cleaning it off my face, I obviously drifted into it! Tashi is also at the tent entrance, asking me about money.

"How much money did you say? I can't understand why you want it." I am confused by the conversation.

"I need $250 U.S. The only way you can continue is on a pony, just to take you over the high pass tomorrow."

"I thought we had covered the high pass today." I am trying to be funny, but it is missing the mark!

"That amount will leave me almost penniless until we get back to Kathmandu." Dear Rainy comes to the rescue.

"I can loan you $100."

Tashi collects the money and disappears into the night. I will never forget what he did that night; walking down the mountain in the dead of night, then back up, to save me from being taken back to Darchen. Drifting in and out of sleep, my mind is in a whirlpool of thoughts and dreams. I had considered, before I left New Zealand, that I might die on this trip. A concept that had not frightened me and one I was ready to accept. Now I feel as close to death as one could ever get, and I am not so sure that I want to finish my life at this moment. My two sons don't even know that I am here, and then there are all the cats. One day I hope to be back here, spend more time in Lhasa, and other areas of Tibet. So now is not such a good time to die!

MONDAY JUNE 8TH

"I am relieved you are still with us." I hear Rainy's voice. Her face comes slowly into focus.

"You were rambling on about having a heart attack, Ramesh is very worried." My lungs are gasping for air, with the consequence of a prolonged coughing fit. Ramesh appears armed with Ibuprofen and insists I start antibiotics. They leave me in peace, but on the promise that I will make it to the mess tent for breakfast. The frozen landscape comes as rather a surprise, but as we are over 5000 metres I should have expected it. The yaks are being rounded up in readiness for the day's trek. Enthusiastic trekkers pass our camp with huge powerful strides and walking sticks already in a set rhythm. There are no chairs or tables, but everyone is in a buoyant mood, and the hot tea and porridge is a welcome sight. I stay on after the rest of the group return to the tents to pullout the holdalls ready for loading. In search of more tea I find the next tent is the cooking tent, and the gas burner offers welcome warmth. Suddenly, all hell breaks loose. I am bowled off the box that has been my seat, and rolled over several

times, by the burly Nepali cook. Spitting out dirt and stones, gasping for breath I manage to let out a shout.

"What the hell are you doing?"

"Madam, you are on fire!"

I finally come to rest amidst broken bags of lentils, rice and noodles, with the cook still beating my right side. There are feathers everywhere, and a couple of startled, but amused locals are looking in. The oversize down coat now has a large hole down the lower right side, and exudes handfuls of feathers on my every movement. There is an awful, cremated smell, both in the tent and about my person. My first thought is Ramesh. He is going to be furious. The cook helps me up and we investigate the damage. By now the tent is full of the camp staff and a vigorous discussion ensues as to how to repair the hole. The best we can do is to bunch the gaping hole together and tie it with twine. Enter Ramesh! Most of the explanation is done by the cook in Nepalese, probably a good thing as I can't understand what is being said. I summon my deepest apology and put on a helpless look. Well, I do look rather wretched and I am still shaking noodles out of my hair, which sets off another explosion of feathers despite the repair. As I exit the cook tent to find Tashi and the pony I ooze feathers. Naturally when the rest of the group see me coming there is hysterical laughter.

"Well we won't lose you anymore, just look for the feathers." I hear Saumya call out. Tashi is trying to stifle his giggles, and we get on with the job of sorting out the pony.

He has come back with two, one for Ferris also, plus the accompanying horsemen. I am allocated a small grey mare, about 14 hands. I have ridden before, many years ago. There is no saddle, just a wooden seat covered over with a piece of Tibetan carpet. The stirrup irons are held on with extremely short rope, however there is a bridle of sorts. Everyone looks on waiting for my next disaster; they are to be disappointed! I am up in the saddle with no assistance and amazingly feel right at home. Even Tashi is surprised with how easy I am finding this. Ferris, on the other hand, is having great difficulty just mounting. When they do finally get him mounted, he looks like a sack of potatoes, and very unsure about the whole experience. Most of the other ponies have been taken by Indian women, some rather overweight. For the first time I notice that many of them are still wearing their saris under the standard issue clothing.

The yaks move out in their lumbering style and the horsemen lead the ponies through the start of a precarious ride. I know the best thing is to give plenty of slack rein and lean forward. With the stirrups so short I am riding jockey style, but I soon get the hang of it. It is remarkable how the pony picks her way between huge boulders, finding the narrowest of crevices to place her hooves. I am really enjoying this and can understand why I needed the ride. The ascent is brutal, and we are climbing to a height of 5,900 metres—over 18,000 feet! The scenery is spectacular. I have the north face of Kailash to my right and now negotiate the heart of the Dolma La Pass. There are one or two places where I have to dismount, the ground being so treacherous. This is proving to be one of the highlights of my day. Tashi has stayed with me the whole way. Ferris and Tenzin have fallen someway behind, and the rest of the group have unbelievably overtaken us and are nowhere to be seen. It has become

almost a race with some of them, to see who can complete the day's trek first. Susan has been jogging in parts.

We finally reach the top of the pass after about one and a half hours. It plateaus out and suddenly the magnitude of where I am hits home. I thank the horseman, and cup the mare's muzzle in my hands. She has been wonderful. I have talked to her most of the way as without her I would certainly not be here. Tashi and I sit on a rock and share the packed lunch, followed by a shared smoke. The trekkers march on past seemingly unconcerned enough with sheer beauty of the surroundings to stop. All Tibetans picnic here, as it is customary to leave a piece of one's clothing as an offering to the mountain. A sea of prayer flags stretch out as far as the eye can see. I am immersed in a giant rainbow, being held aloft by the hands of Kailash. Joining the locals I tie a silk bag containing a small Buddha, another photo of the Karmapa and a *khata*. These were given to me by Christine, the manager Of Karma Choeling Temple back in New Zealand with the request that I leave them here. I have prayer flags and *khatas* from Lhasa, and a sock representing my offering. Sadly the accumulation of litter blowing amongst the rocks emphasizes that this is now more of a tourist vacation than a Buddhist pilgrimage.

Finally Ferris, Tenzin and Lakpa arrive. Waiting for them to have a rest and some food gives me the chance to finally take some photographs. I have given up with the big Fuji camera for now, preferring the tiny pocket Kodak camera, a gift from my son Daniel. It weighs nothing and slips easily into my coat pocket. Ten minutes later we start out, heading for our second night on the mountain. I have lost my sunglasses and lip balm,

with the consequence that my lips are like coarse grade sandpaper, and my eyes are very sore. The wind has sprung up and the temperature is dropping fast. There is still plenty of clambering over boulders, small rises and falls, and ice. Two Indian gentlemen stop and carry me up one of the steeper parts. As I thank them, my eye is attracted over their shoulders toward what looks like a block of ice in a rock recess. Not sure if I am imagining things or if the high altitude is playing tricks, I am looking at Lord Shiva.

The descent is becoming more obvious as I am now able to walk further between rests. The five of us have stayed together since the Dolma Pass. Coming down the far side of the pass is the Tukje Tso, or Compassionate Lake. The mountain face towers above the campsite which finally comes into view. We are camped on a sheet of ice, somewhat different to the tour guide notes which describe our second night as "camping on grassy slopes beneath the spectacular rock cliffs." I still have issues with sleeping, and with a drop in temperature to —12 degrees, this night is proving to be the worst. Rainy is very patient but finally snaps: "When was the last time you camped?"

"Never!" is my answer between coughing spasms.

"You have never been camping?" I can hear that familiar tone of disbelief in her voice.

"I went to France as a toddler, where we camped for a week, but that tent had two bedrooms, beds, and all the bells and whistles. It was also a good deal warmer."

I hear the snow fall during the night, and hope we don't get up to a large dump.

TUESDAY JUNE 9th

Sleeping in the coat has proved to be rather a disaster as I have feathers everywhere. The fresh snow is not too much but, my goodness, it is cold! The group are huddled together in the mess tent. As I appear the conversation turns to me. Evidently I now have the name of Calamity Jane due to my unexpected riding skills. None of them would have undertaken riding a pony in this terrain, so I have scored some points! Ferris informs us that an Indian woman fell from her horse and had to be stretched down with a broken ankle. I soon lose the points when I come under criticism from Ramesh for not disclosing the fact that I have no camping experience. Rainy has been telling tales!

This is the last day of the *khora*, rather sad, as I am now feeling much better and more acclimatised to the altitude and conditions. The main group race away at speed leaving Ferris, Tenzin, Lakpa, Tashi and I to make the descent at our own pace. On the left, the river is far below the cliff face. The sun is up, catching the water and turning it into a myriad of diamonds. Tashi and I go on ahead, and he starts singing:

> "I am sailing. I am sailing, home again, across the sea, I am sailing, forever sailing, to be near you, to be free. Can you hear me, can you hear me, across the dark clouds, far away. I am crying, forever crying, to be near you, to be free."

I give him a big smile. This is his version of the Rod Stewart song. We begin to bump shoulders in fun, like a couple of kids. I try to join him in the song which he is repeating, but nothing comes out of my mouth. Breathing is still difficult. The warmth of the sun is nowhere near the strength of warmth that radiates between us. Suddenly the shoulder bumping becomes quite a hefty push. As I turn to face him, I see the reason behind the sudden change. A herd of yaks is headed straight for us. We are on quite a narrow track, with a long drop to the left and a rocky outcrop to the right. Not too many places to run! There are eight of them, forming a hairy horizontal line of unstoppable power. There is one large boulder, precariously close to the edge; we make a dash for it. Crouching low behind the rock, they lumber past. The one nearest is so close I feel its body heat. Yaks are the camels of the Himalayas. Their hair, skin and meat are all put to good use. The females, or *dri*, supply the milk for the famous Tibetan butter tea. They can carry enormous loads, and live in this inhospitable environment comfortably. I am told that if they descend to less than 4,000 metres they die. They need the altitude to survive.

We continue our journey toward the small monastery of Zutrul Puk and the Miracle cave of Milarepa.

"I can't get up there." is my response to the proposed visit to the monastery and cave.

"Yes you can, we will go very slowly." Tashi takes my arm and we start a twenty minute climb."

I am glad for the encouragement as I would have been cross with myself had I not

come up here. The commentaries of Milarepa are by far some of my favourite reading. The book I have with me is "Drinking the Mountain Stream" a recently published selection of his verse. He is widely recognized as Tibet's beloved Saint, living a simple life here in these mountains. Born in 1040, Milarepa's life followed the theme of transforming from sinner, through the Dharma—teachings of Buddha, to Saint. Shunning typical adornments usually bestowed on such an important figure, he wore a simple white cotton drape. Repa means "cotton clad" hence the addition to his name of Mila. It is said he turned green due to his excessive consumption of nettles. He is the disciple of Marpa, one of the forerunners of the Kagyu lineage of Tibetan Buddhism. Kagyu translates as "the ear whisperers", as much of the lineage teaching is done through oral transmission. Most portraits of Milarepa have him seated in the lotus position, cupping his right ear with his hand. It is a wonderful experience to actually find myself standing and prostrating in such a special place.

We have about another two hours walking ahead, thankfully downhill all the way. I feel exuberant, and am negotiating the track like a mountain goat. In the distance Lake Manasarovar is in full view. The valley below opens up with the vista disappearing into infinity.

We come across two women who are prostrating the entire journey. They use small animal bones to mark where their outstretched arms and fingers lay in the dirt. This is where they place their feet for the next one. It will take a minimum of three weeks to complete their circumambulation. Ramesh has remarked that he intends to walk barefoot on the next tour he brings, which I find quite surprising. He and I have heated conversations about his apparent support for the Chinese, and his condemnation of the protests conducted by the Tibetan refugees in his home country, Nepal. I have one more task to finish this journey; to take some of the earth. Tashi is reading my mind, and pulls me to a stop.

"Here is the place to take the earth from. It is red, like that of dried yak blood, called Dronkpa."

He gives me a small bag.

"How much should I take?"

"Take as much or as little as you think you need."

I find a hollow that has been scraped out over hundreds of years, by the fingers of men women and children and once more the tears fall. I take enough for Thuten—President of Friends of Tibet in New Zealand, Lama Pasang, myself, and His Holiness The Dalai Lama. I have brought an empty paper bag, printed with "Mud face pack from Rotorua" which I intend to use to get this through the stiff New Zealand environment rules at the airport. Hopefully it will get through without being zapped by the fumigation process. As I tuck the little package into one of the deep pockets of the coat, my hand finds the two coins given to me by the lady with the locks in Dharamsala. Instantly I know one of these is for Tashi. It takes him a moment to realize what is in my hand as I offer him the coin. Then I see the expression of recognition.

"I can't take this from you."

My hand goes back into the pocket for the other one.

"I have two identical, they are not both for me." I press one of them into the palm of his hand. I know he realizes the significance of this gesture as he closes his fingers around the coin.

Once we arrive at the sort of bus station for yaks and ponies I know we are nearing the end. This is a mini-settlement and some of the tents are the typical nomad style made from yak skin. It is buzzing with activity. Tashi knows his way round and directs us to the tea tent. At last some real warmth, this time safely enclosed within the traditional tin heat-box. Feathers are still finding their freedom from my coat, albeit now in ones and twos. Most of the stuffing from the right side has gone. One single feather, once a small part of a much larger whole, takes flight high up in the mountain, riding the winds, falling with the snow, resting in the caves to join with the spirits; my everlasting offering to the sacred mountain. At least that will be my explanation to the tour company manager! At last a cup of butter tea. So far on this trip all I have had is black tea and, a now dwindling, supply of Nescafe.

It is nearing mid afternoon by the time we round the last bend. The customary wind has whipped up a storm of shale and sand. I have learned over the last three days to make a face mask out of my scarf which afford some protection. Peering through he dust I can make out the Land Cruisers and trucks waiting at the side of the road. A line of figures are in front, and as Tashi and I get closer I hear clapping and cheering. We are being greeted with a rapturous welcome, lots of hugs and "Well done." I am quite overwhelmed, burst into tears and give Tashi a big hug. As we get into the vehicles I catch a glimpse of myself in the wing mirror. Oh my goodness what a sight! My eyes are burned red raw with the lack of protection; my lips look like a wire brush; I have feathers protruding from all over the place. I have been walking and sleeping in the same clothes for 5 or 6 days. The outer casing of my gloves has shredded revealing the padding; the right side of my coat is in tatters. I could almost be mistaken for one of the wrathful deities. Apart from all that I am in good spirits, relieved I made it, and pleased to sit down on a seat.

As we speed off toward Lake Manasarovar I look back at Kailash retreating behind us. Not once until we arrived did I contemplate what I was taking on. I do know that it is the dream of so many to be here and never make it. Am I lucky, especially in the circumstance of no preparation, inadequate clothing etc to have completed the *khora*? There is no such thing as luck; causes and conditions, *karma,* yes! Maybe I have waited many lifetimes to come back home. I do know that Kailash was kind to me. We have already been informed that 12 people did not reach the finish, including a Chinese soldier. The cremation site has been busy. Lake Manasarovar, on the opposite side to where we were, is quite different. An awful concrete lodge complex has been built for the Indian pilgrims. Most of the group seems happy to stay in camp until dinner. For me it is a question of which is the better of the two evils: the tent or more walking. I decide to walk.

A small flock of sheep are in the distance and I can see at least one person in attendance.

As I get closer in the hope that I might have a chat, I see it is a woman with a small girl, probably her daughter. The sheep are startled by my appearance, so it is better to keep my distance. I watch them being rounded up with no more than whistles from the woman. One or two make a break for it and the small girl, armed with a catapult loaded with a clod of mud, at the speed of light lets fly. She is a perfect shot. She hits one of the sheep on the rear, and the message is heeded. Both sheep return to the flock. It is a slow process, but no one is in a hurry. I spot a lamb that has become detached, do they know? The flock carry on, leaving the lamb behind, I am about to stand and draw their attention to it, when the small girl rushes back. She picks up the straggler and carries it some distance to the safety of it's mother. Watching her struggle with a creature nearly as big as herself is tearing at my instinct to help. It would be wrong to interfere. It is time to go back to camp. A strong, cold wind has blown up making the walk back hard work. Dinner is a mammoth affair as we have been living on essentials only, for the last three days. Returning to the mess tent when all is quiet is a chance to stand under the huge moon and millions of stars. Kailash, with a fresh fall of snow, glistens under the night sky. For me, she has become the face of Tibet.

WEDNESDAY JUNE 10TH

As a consequence of a raging dust storm in the night, we are covered in dust and grit. It has penetrated every crevice and orifice, and has not helped my extremely sore eyes. The pace of the packing up and start has slowed considerably, bordering on the leisurely. This gives me a chance to have a smoke with Tashi and ask him about Kailash's guardians, as I have called them.

"The mountain is named Gurla Mandhata, the protector of Kailash. The Chinese have an army in there, somewhere. Many thousands of soldiers"

I am not sure if he means actually in the mountain somehow or simply hidden behind it. What gives me a warm glow is the fact that my instinctive feel of the mountain's role was right. Momentarily the "how did I know" pops into my head but the fact that the Chinese now use that protection for their own destructive purposes, has the opposite effect, giving me a cold shudder.

There is one more thing I have to do before we leave. Fill one of my plastic water bottles with water from the lake. This I hope will travel with me, much the same as the earth, back to New Zealand. The water is freezing, there are no cranes, and the area in general is quite dirty from the piles of rubbish being scattered by the wind. There is an Indian gentleman up to his waist in the water, busy washing his hair; the shampoo suds forming a scum on the lake surface. How many more years of tourist abuse can these Holy places endure, before they, like the Tibetans themselves, become irretrievably lost?

Finally we are on our way to visit Chiu Gompa or the Bird Monastery, some distance around the lake. The first thing I notice is the giant communication dish sited just behind the monastery. It is rather a sad backdrop to the wheel of dharma and the two deer that are still situated on the highest point, looking out over the Holy Lake. At least this one

is still here, unlike all the other Gompas that used to be dotted around the lake. They are no more than piles of stones, finding their way back into the ground, from where they originated.

It is a precarious climb to the top with many of the stone steps and walking ledges crumbling away. There is just one old monk, collecting monetary offerings. It is time to part company with the group; easy to do with the numerous little alley ways. Most of the doors are original but bear the weight of hefty padlocks and notices in Chinese. This is reputedly the site of a cave where Padmasambhava or Guru Rinpoche, lived for the last seven years of his life. It is rather sad that the Gompa should end its life padlocked and empty. Gompas are traditionally small monasteries, with the emphasis on the practice of deep meditation. Sometimes they can amount to no more than a meditation room.

Lake Manasarovar is a brilliant turquoise, the air is calm and the feel of the stone warm to the touch. The peace is soon disturbed by the group clattering down the steps time to leave. I feel the urge to hide behind the mass of prayer flags and let them go without me, in the hope that they won't notice I am missing. Foolish plan!

A short drive brings us to the thermal pools. The smell of sulphur is quite overpowering, but the water is gloriously warm. A local entrepreneur has built individual bath houses, for which he is charging an exorbitant fee for a twenty minute soak. Karen, Saumya, Susan and Tash all take the offer up, leaving the rest of us to dip our feet in the big open pools for free. Back on the road, once again into the moonscape of sand dunes; we stop several times for the convoy to re-group. This always gives Tashi and I a chance to walk along the road and share a smoke. Trouble is whereas I had got it down to about four a day, the number is back on the increase. It is on one of these breaks that we talk about the Dalai Lama.

"Have you met Him?" is Tashi's question.

"Not exactly, I have had the good fortune to go to three of his teachings when He came to New Zealand. I have many DVDs of His teachings. Do you ever dream of the day when He will return to Tibet?"

"This is never possible."

I see that sense of hopelessness return to his face:

"If it were possible to give him a letter, what would you say?". My mind is thinking that as I already know His Holiness is due to visit New Zealand six months after my return, I could include a letter with the other things I plan to present, if I get the chance.

"There is not much to say. I would just write—what do we do? What do we do?"

The bottom of my stomach feels as though it has dropped out on hearing this simple and pitiful plea for help. We link arms on the way back to the trucks, and he starts his Rod Stewart song again. This time I am able to accompany him.

We stop to watch two women milking a flock of sheep. They have an amazing way of looping their horns together to prevent them from running away. The women do not take much notice of us. I can't resist getting closer and sticking my fingers into the pail of frothing warm milk; absolutely delicious. The woman looks up momentarily and our eyes engage. Once again that overwhelming warmth and recognition ignites, and she gives me a big smile.

"Tho che chey", thank you, is all I have for her.

As we slow for yet another stop, I can't believe my eyes, a petrol station. The first we have come across since leaving Shigatse, which seems forever. It is hardly a Shell station and there is certainly no coffee and muffins! However there is a toilet block, which prompts some enthusiastic cheers. Cheers that are short-lived. I get sent in first to investigate, {why me!}. The waiting, expectant faces are suddenly downcast when they see the look on my face as I exit. It is back to a convenient rock or, in this case, a wall!

We have been on the road for nearly six hours and had to suffer two long wait police check points. It is quite late before we find a campsite. Obviously all the overnight stops have to be close to water. This particular spot has a wide margin of boggy ground between the road and the stream, impossible for the vehicles to cross. Once again we are camped on the side of the road, with verdant green pasture around us. The mountains continue to be our neighbours, altogether quite a peaceful setting. The usual daily wind is late arriving, giving us time to eat dinner without the customary buffeting. I stay on, as usual, to write up my notes, whilst the others retreat to their tents. The next few moments happen with such speed it is difficult to recall accurately. One minute I am sitting in the deserted mess tent absorbed in the day's events, the next moment both the large tent, table, chairs and me are airborne and being catapulted some distance. I come to rest still inside the tent which is now a huge jumble of canvas, ropes and furniture. There are people rushing about outside.

"Jane, Jane, are you OK?"

"Yes I'm OK. I don't know how to get out." After some pulling and unraveling I am freed from the tent and emerge to find everyone in hysterical laughter. I think Saumya nearly had an accident, as there were tears of laughter running down her face.

"There is no way I'm using the toilet tent tonight!" are my first words.

After that initial gust, the wind abates just a little. Sleeping in the igloo was even more of a nightmare than usual, and with the mess tent left in its partially dismantled state I almost considered getting in the back of one of the support trucks, along with the cook!

THURSDAY JUNE 11TH

The dust storm prevailed most of the night with the consequence that the camp is covered in sand, and I have the most vicious headache. We have dropped to around 4,400 metres and the temperature is warmer. I have come to the conclusion that the headaches are

more the result of hours being thrown about in the Land Cruiser than the altitude. Ramesh's supply of Iburofen is nearly exhausted, my own stock finished days ago. As we pack up I notice we have been joined by two curious horsemen and their ponies. They are keeping their distance on the opposite side of the road. With a quick glance to assess if I will be missed, I go to join the two nomads. The ponies are skitterish, but the two men are welcoming. We don't say anything. They chat to each other giving me periodic, quizzical looks. The "I wish" swallows reality, as I see myself galloping across the Tibetan plateau, free from the shackles of being "on tour". More probable, considering the reality of the situation here, I would be hanging around in Darchen waiting for the next tourist that can't walk the Dolma Pass unaided! My own reality comes back with bellows from the camp crew.

"Jane, we're going!"

"Please go without me" is my silent response, as I bid the riders farewell.

Two hours into the drive, disaster strikes. Smoke is pouring from the front wheels of our Land Cruiser. The convoy has become staggered, and we only have one other of the vehicles in sight. Finding a good place to pull over, work starts on finding the cause of the problem. It is bad news. The front bearings have gone and, worse still, so has the rear stub axle. Within half an hour the convoy has re-grouped and the customary analysis of the situation begins. Ramesh is not pleased. It is quite clear that the fitness of the vehicles is down to the Tibetans prior to the journey commencing. He is responsible for the camping side of things as well as the schedule. I have learned there is one thing that annoys Ramesh—it is falling behind the timetable. We settle down for a long wait. Our temporary site is on the banks of a wide, but shallow river. The water is crystal clear with fish in abundance. Brilliant sunshine is now penetrating the earlier cold. A lazy feeling nestles us into the comfort of its warm blanket. For the first time since Darchen, I feel confident enough to remove the yak sweater. It is like parting company with a good friend, and a friend it most certainly has been. The natural oils have kept out the damp whilst the weight of the wool buffered the cold wind. Saumya comes to sit with me, we chat about the journey, then find ourselves flat out on the hard Tibetan earth, sunbathing.

As time passes, the euphoria of relaxing gives way to restlessness; Susan has already taken off on some hike, or another shot of gin! We make our way along the river to find a family making bricks out of the shale and mud. They have wooden molds which are simply filled to the top with this gloop. Left in the sun to dry and harden, they are turned out, stacked and ready for building with. Yak dung patties are used both for burning in the cooking stove and roof construction on many dwellings. Continuing we come across the family home, complete with a pair of dried ram's balls hanging in the doorway to drive off evil spirits. Thinking of how my customers back at the cattery would react if I had the same protection over the office door gives me the giggles.

Finally the vehicle horn sounds, the signal that we can recommence our journey. It has taken four hours to sort the problem out. Unbelievably we only drive about thirty kilometres before we arrive in a small, tatty settlement and now stop for the drivers and crew to have lunch. They disappear into a roadside dwelling leaving the group unsure

what to do next. Tenzin and Ferris have disappeared, so I tag on with the girls who have found a general store. It is more like a liquor store, dozens of boxes containing bottled beer line the back wall. Immediately they are talking party! This is not really my idea of fun, so I retrace my steps looking for Tashi and the crew. When I find them, Tashi ensures I have a seat, a bowl of tsampa, and Tibetan tea. The room is large and resembles a bric-à-brac store. It is full of everything, from huge wonderful old Tibetan cabinets, tables, chests, carpets, to trinket boxes. Two women are serving the men, arriving from another part of the building with bowls of steaming noodles, tsampa, and tea. One of them opens a cupboard and pulls out a large dried rib bone. It looks to be well over a foot long, and is passed around each man who somehow pulls off a chunk of meat with his teeth. It arrives in my lap. Fortunately everyone is engrossed in the TV, showing what looks to be a Chinese soap opera, so they don't notice my lack of enthusiasm or ability to pull my share. Gaba takes it back and cuts a piece off with a huge knife, giving me the piece before sending the bone around for a second time. I will be chewing this until the end of time. It is like trying to chew and swallow an old shoe. Spitting it out would be discourteous, so I tuck it into my cheek until we get outside and I can quietly dispose of it. As I sit, with ancient dried yak meat pushing my cheek out enough to resemble a large facial boil, I run my gaze over smaller objects that are crammed into any available space; cheap Chinese ornaments, autographed photos of tourists, bits of clothing and of all things a pot of 'Whitening cleansing Milk Contains snake skin oil'. There is clearly a desire to lighten the fairly dark Tibetan complexion, in keeping with the Chinese.

Once outside I look for a suitable place to dispose of the yak meatball, but not before I am noticed by Saumya.

"What happened to your face?" she cannot contain her laughter.

"You don't want to know, it will be OK in a minute."

A huge rubbish tip across the road relieves me of the meat, which is eagerly gobbled up by one of the many street dogs.

So much time has been lost due to the breakdown, the convoy pulls over just six kilometres further down the road. The sand dune giants are our neighbours; it is a desolate spot to camp. Tonight and tomorrow night are the last two under canvas and almost the end of the journey. Any hopes of quiet reflection are scuppered with the decision to have a farewell party. Chinese beer and cigarettes are ridiculously cheap and sadly the Tibetans have resorted to both. With no jobs, their land, culture, language, religion all under progressive threat there is not much else to do. The old adage "drowning our sorrows" comes to mind. I join the others in the mess tent for one beer, before leaving them to it. Being teetotal apart from the odd glass of wine on special occasions, it is difficult to get into the swing. Karen and Greg are certainly no strangers to "knocking it back!"

FRIDAY JUNE 12TH

A giant hangover shrouds the camp. All is quiet until fairly late. Trekkers and crew alike, oblivious to the gale force wind during the night, seem shocked that we are nearly submerged under sand. The mess tent is almost dismantled around us. Ramesh is urgently trying to speed things up. The road surface is improving. There are not so many passes to climb in second gear as we have been doing, and not so many hair-raising descents. The sand stretches for miles. Some of the dwellings we pass are lost under it with just the roof visible. Tashi and Gaba are in a jovial mood, singing songs in Tibetan.

"What are you singing about?" I enquire

"How much we are looking forward to going home to Lhasa," comes Gaba's reply. This arouses my own thoughts of home. Yes, I have missed all my seventeen cats and talking to my sons. But I know I will miss Tibet when it is time to go.

The hours tick by, and there is nothing. It is a vast wilderness with no sign of life. And yet before the Chinese invasion there would have been a monastery, or Gompa, every ten miles or so, seasonal settlements of nomads and their herds; villages, crops, and life. The Chinese have destroyed well over 6,000 Monasteries, both large and small, and that figure is ever increasing. The country has been raped of its precious religious artifacts, scriptures and statues, manyhaving been sold on the international art and antiquities markets. Over two million Tibetans have been slaughtered, mostly from the Monastic community, or Sangha. Hundreds of thousands languish in Chinese prisons, without

charge or trial. Public executions of Tibetans are the highest number in the World. Mining, deforestation, damming of some of the planet's largest rivers whose water is so critical to all of Asia; nuclear waste dumping and general land destruction. These are only a few of the consequences of China taking Tibet. But the most critical element is that China now sits on the heels of what could one day be her most prized jewel—India.

We stop to eat our packed lunch, stretch our legs and for Tashi, Gaba and I to have a chat about their return to Lhasa. We are still at about 4,400 metres, but I hardly notice it any more. Way out in the distance a building can be seen on the pinnacle of a high ridge. Tashi sensing my inquisitiveness remarks:

"It is a small Monastery, quite new, only three monks."

Two figures become visible through the intensity of the sun's rays reflecting off the sand. We wait to see if they come in our direction. As they finally approach, I can identify them as two women. The taller is a young woman, her heavy chuba torn and frayed in places. The other woman is elderly and small. She wears a multi coloured scarf wrapped around her head, but I can see the grey flecked braids protruding at her exposed neckline. She has the most beautiful face that melts into my soul like soft butter. I feel humbled in her presence and am totally captivated by her features. I ask her permission to take photos, the camera seems to have a mind of its own. Click, click, click! I am handling it like a professional. Her skin is a strange colour, so I ask Tashi to explain.

"She has used dried yak blood to give protection against the weather and sand".

We look at the photos on the viewing screen, she chats to me in a soft, gentle voice. Her eyes move from the camera to me; they are pools of liquid amber, moist with tears. Her smile could light up the whole of Tibet. I shall never forget her. Will she forget me?

We continue on what is one of the longest drives in a day, until a small group of stone dwellings come into view. Already it is late afternoon and as we pull off the road I am wondering if we will have a solid roof over our heads. The buildings are deserted, but there is a green paddock behind them, complete with a babbling brook. The next disaster; one of the big support trucks slides off the narrow track leading into the field, and sinks into a sand drift. It is leaning at about a 30 degree tilt to the left. We hear the load in the back crashing for a moment, then all is quiet. This is going to be a challenge getting it out. The now familiar discussion starts, with much hand waving, and raised voices. There isn't enough room for the second truck to assist, and with the unreliability of the Land Cruisers, no one seems to have an answer. We all assist in unloading the vehicle before a tow rope is attached to the best of the three Land Cruisers. The front wheel comes free and onto the track but the rear double wheels look as if they are on ice skates. It takes over an hour with additional ideas to finally free the truck from the sand. A near gale force wind is with us, cloaking everything again in fine sand and shale.

This is our last night with Gaba and the other Tibetan drivers for tomorrow we will be in a hotel in Zhangmu. The cook has stunned us for a second time by arriving in the mess tent with a huge chocolate cake to celebrate our time together. A whip round, collecting the tips has already been done and these are gratefully received. Already I am touched with the sadness of letting go. We have one more day's drive in Tibet then our paths that have crossed on this amazing journey, will once more go their separate ways.

SATURDAY JUNE 13TH

"Rainy, are you awake there is something wrong outside, my side of the tent is being pushed in."

Before she has time to answer, I open the fly zip and am staring up the wet nose of a cow. I wasn't aware that there were cows In Tibet. This is certainly different to Juddha and his "black tea, washing water".

"Rainy, there is a cow outside."

"Don't be silly, there are no cows in Tibet." is her muffled answer from the depths of her sleeping bag.

I look again—no cow. I know I didn't imagine a cow, so emerge further from the tent. Yes, we are surrounded by cows!

"Rainy, there is a herd of cows. You'll see when you get up."

The animals seem as bemused as the two girls tending them. They too peer into

every tent chuckling to themselves. There is a frost on the ground, the air crisp, with a clear blue sky.

Once breakfast is over, the camping gear is loaded for the last time. Our destination is Saga, then on through the Sun Kosi Gorge to Zhangmu, the border town between Tibet and Nepal. The sand is retreating, as we enter the southern part of the plateau. The mountains now run parallel with us; a range that includes Shishapangma with a summit of 8012 metres. Tashi points out three magnificent peaks known as "The Three Brothers". Thankfully we stop for a photo shoot. It is on one of these stops that we bump into another small group of horsemen. The elder has the most amazing hairdo; braids leave his scalp at right angles. One would think he had a gale force wind blowing it that way, but no, it stands like that of its own accord. Similar to the old lady yesterday his smile and look reflect the kindness that is at the core of these people. He has a front tooth missing, and his face is a canvas of deep furrows and crevices, similar to the face of the mountains in the distance behind him. Old turquoise and coral hang from his ears. His Western style clothes have seen better days. They have resorted to using their ponies for tourists to sit on for that photo of: "This is me in Tibet."

As we are about to leave I hand him ten yuan and try to explain that I don't need the photo of "Me in Tibet" to take home. I will always be here, in my heart, in my mind.

According to the tour itinerary we are supposed to be crossing the Tsangpo river by ferry. Having already passed one huge hydroelectric dam, I can only assume that this is the reason for not needing a ferry. Still on every bridge we cross the hundreds of prayer flags continue with their message. Tibetans, no matter where they are be it here or abroad, will never give up the fight to have their country returned. The prayer flags are very much a symbol of that belief.

We descend into the town of Saga, and the tragedy of Tibet hits like a hundred pound cannon ball. Being up in the mountains made it possible for these scenes to be cast aside. Now we are back amidst the devastation. Block after block of concrete, the apartment homes of the Han Chinese. A high street still under construction, boasting new Chinese hotels, grocery stores, and restaurants. It is all badly planned, mostly unfinished with piles of rubbish festering on any available piece of empty ground. Karen finally voices what has been running through the minds of most of us:

"This is a shit hole, a dump!"

Ramesh takes us to a Tibetan restaurant for lunch, and informs us that we have to wait for a permit to pass through the Gorge. Evidently it is one way traffic only, four hours one way and four the opposite. It seems we have just missed our open period and now face a four hour wait.

After some hot food, everyone feels a lot better. At least the weather is still good for wandering the streets of this hell hole. There are a couple of Tibetan-run shops selling clothing, khatas and the like. It is in one of these that I find the most beautiful pair of handmade boots. These are not the festival style, just the everyday type. I have noticed that very few people wear them any more; most wear cheap Chinese trainers or similar.

The shopkeeper refuses to budge on the price, and the hire of the pony has left finances a little tight.

Frustration is setting in, especially with Ferris and Karen. As we wait by the vehicles for a sign that we are going, Saumya starts to try and give away some of her personal items, including the Chanel sunglasses. Her spare pair of gloves and a scarf are snapped up by the locals that have now gathered anxious to see what is on offer. However the prized sunglasses are rejected out of hand. Poor Saumya, she is quite hurt that no one wants them, especially as they probably cost more that what the average a Tibetan earns in six months. Many of the *malas* and bracelets she has purchased are eagerly accepted. One particular turquoise and coral bracelet she gives to an older lady that has been to shy to come forward with the rest of the population that are eager for a free gift. The woman talks quickly, accompanied by hand signals. A shopkeeper comes out to translate.

"She wants you to stay here for a few moments, she has something to give you, please wait."

She returns and hands Saumya an identical brass disc that was given to me in Darchen. Mine has been in my pocket since it was given to me, and I now pull it out.

"Saumya, I have one, given to me in Darchen."

Gaba and the other drivers have appeared wondering what all the excitement is about. They seem particularly interested in the, now two, identical discs.

"What is their meaning?" I ask.

"They are protection for you," is Gaba's reply. Well they seemed to have spurred Ramesh into action as we get the convoy underway, after just two hours of waiting. We have to stop for Ferris's bladder only a short distance from the town. I look back to the appalling sight it casts on what was probably a beautiful horizon. Practically underfoot, I catch a glimpse of blue on the ground. A tiny wild Iris, so perfect, so fragile, is growing in nothing but dust and stones. Even more surprising, I catch sight of a butterfly. The two more, than likely, are dependent on each other in this bleak environment.

As we start the descent toward the Gorge, it begins to rain. This is the first rain I have felt since the hailstorm back in McLeod Ganj, forever ago! The road narrows to just a single lane, with hairpin bends every few kilometres. The landscape is changing dramatically to green. The Bhute Kosi river, hundreds of feet below us, is a raging torrent of whitewater and rapids. The towering cliffs create a cavernous feeling, accentuated by the dimming light and damp musty air. Suddenly we grind to a halt. Before us, perched on the narrow road between heaven and hell, is a long queue of trucks, minibuses, cars and four-wheel drives. It is already near four o'clock in the afternoon, and we are now informed the road is closed until six o' clock. It is a long two hours. Sitting in the vehicle for short periods is OK, but even though the chilly damp conditions are beginning to bite, walking up and down the road is preferable. A spectacular, waterfall cascades down the cliff face above us. A concrete canopy has been built to protect the road, the water hits it with a crash before leaping off to continue its fall to the river. Heavy clouds roll in enveloping us in their

sodden core. At times all visibility is lost, when it is advisable to stay clear of the edge.

It is dark before we get the green light to proceed, and the most treacherous part of the entire journey begins. Whether the Chinese are repairing huge landslips or still constructing the road is difficult to ascertain. There is no road, just deep mud. The makeshift tents of the workers hang by a thread along the edge of the precipice. Earthmoving equipment is still working under huge arc lights. The Land Cruiser slips and slides to such a degree we are forced to hang onto the backs of the front seats. Ferris is nearly having a nervous breakdown, demanding to be let out of the vehicle. The rear wheels are fighting to get a grip on something, and several times we only just escape being bogged down. For the first time on this trip I am a little frightened. We catch glimpses of the drop below; my stomach is in my mouth. The windscreen wipers desperately try to clear the mud from the screen. It becomes so bad, Gaba is forced to drive with his door open to have some vision. The minutes tick by and slowly the road starts to harden. We are out of the worst. Twenty minutes further on the convoy re-groups and Ramesh does the rounds ensuring all are OK. Ferris's response is not printable. Susan did get out of the second vehicle and walked, insisting she felt far safer—probably right. Meryl is intending to contact the tour company, and in no uncertain terms advise that this part of future trips be cancelled, and an alternative be found. Tempers and nerves are running high. I take my hat off to Gaba. His driving skills were unbelievable, the consequences had he failed, are terrifying to say the least.

It is eight o'clock by the time we reach Zhangmu, and our woes are far from over! The town is built on the side of a hill, not dissimilar to McLeod Ganj. There is one road that zigzags through the town and this seems to be a giant lorry park, from top to bottom. Hundreds of them reducing the road to one lane and causing havoc. The two big support trucks have the most problems, so we go ahead without them. It takes nearly an hour to cover half the distance to our hotel. Ramesh orders everyone to carry hand luggage and walk the rest of the way. We are led through a labyrinth of stepped passageways, and at last a hotel. Now it is 9 o' clock and the Chinese state-owned boarding house has hot water from 8pm until 10pm. There is a mad dash to the rooms and the showers. Heaven, albeit intermittent, warm water! I let it run over my head wallowing in every drop. The holdalls have yet to arrive, not that I have much in the way of clean clothes in it. No matter, I am clean for the first time since Shigatse, June 1$^{st.}$ A late meal is organized in the restaurant opposite. Seeing dozens of Tibetan women trawling the streets as money changers is a sad end to the day.

Later in the night, with the large window open, the old net curtain hangs like a discarded wedding veil from an arranged marriage between Tibetans and Han Chinese, that simply has not worked. Rainy is sleeping as I watch the twinkling lights of the town; forest-clad mountains behind and stretching down to the valley below. Not a prayer flag in sight. Today, is my son Matthew's birthday. Happy birthday I whisper, love you, miss you, and blow the message, with a kiss, to the stars.

SUNDAY JUNE 14TH

I burrow under the blankets. It can't be time to get up, even though I think I have been sharing with bed bugs. Breakfast is a solemn occasion; I pick at the food, simply not hungry. Gaba is in good spirits, giving out lots of hugs as he loads the Land Cruiser for the last time. We have a six kilometre drive to the border and Friendship Bridge which will take us back to Nepal. The traffic chaos is worse than last night, so once again half the journey is done on foot. Porters have been hired to carry the large holdalls. A massive glass and concrete building stands as the official exit from Tibet—well China—as we are encouraged to comply with. It is packed full of Indians laden down with enormous quantities of Chinese goods; TVs, rice cookers, portable air conditioning units are just some of the boxes I can identify. They seem to have been given preference with the authorities in the processing of exit permits. We wait for two hours. Tashi has come with us leaving Gaba and the other two drivers to wait for his return. A large outdoor viewing platform has been constructed, for friends and family to farewell those who can cross the border. It is only Tibetans who stand there, waving to a group that is now in Nepal. The bridge crosses the Bhute Kosi river, with a span of a mere fifty metres.

Finally we get the call to move through Customs and Immigration, and now wait at the police checkpoint. They will only allow so many to cross at a given time. Tashi bids farewell to the group, thanking them for their patience and feels that we are one of the best groups he has taken. I hang back, wishing I was invisible. It hasn't really sunk in that this is it, the end. He comes over and we hug. As our cheeks touch the same words come from both of us simultaneously in a whisper, words I will never forget:

"I shall miss you"

I have been saving my last English cigarette for him, and as we let go I put it in his hand, he smiles. Our fingers entwine for a second, before he turns and is lost in the crowd.

The fifty metres walk across the bridge has to be the most painful I have experienced. I sing his Rod Stewart song, quietly to myself as I watch the torrent of water below. Once across I look back to the viewing platform, searching for his face. My eyes scan the crowd, please let him be there. Over and over I try to find him, but he has gone.

I recall words from the Buddha Shakyamuni.

"Do not dwell in the past or dream of the future".

The Jokhang

The shambles of the Barkhor

Pilgrim

More Destruction of Lhasa

Tibetan Quarter. Lhasa

View from hotel. Lhasa

The Barkhor and Juniper burning

The Barkhor

The Potala Palace

View from Potala. Monlith in celebration of Chairman Mao

Ascent to the Potala entrance

Dreprung. So much destroyed

Woman. Deprung

Deprung. Some Reconstruction

Deprung

Some history remains

Abandoned but not forgotten

Norbulingka. The Summer Palace

Monk

Only a glimpse of the interior. Norbulingka

Nun. Sera

Monks debting. Sera

Yamdrok So or Torquoise Lake

Yak for photo hire

Local Transport. Gyantse

Pushed to the edge in their homeland

Gyantse

Monastery as garaging

Kubum

Protector deities. Kubum

Protector deities. Kubum

Protector deities. Kubum

Protector deities. Kubum

Guru Rinpoche or Padmasambhava

The decay of Shigatse

The decay of Shigatse

Stupas at Shigatse

Friends. Apron denotes she is married

Entrance to Shigatse. Middle stairs for Panchen Lama only

Recent renovations for the Chinese appointed Panchen Lama

213

Picknicking. Shigatse

Monks numbers reduced to a handful

More destruction

Yamdrok So

Road building by hand

Desertification is visible

The Himalayas. Ngari Region

Lake Manasarovar and Gurla Mandhata

Author in the -dead dog hat-

Pole Raising tarboche

Pole in position

Resentment and hopelessness

Traditional dress

The Sangha

Ready to Go

Gompa. Lake Manasarovar

Trader and Greg. Tarboche

Mt. Kailash

Base camp. Mt. Kailash

The Sangha performing the ceremony

Start of the Khora

Top of the Dolma Pass

My transport

Hanging over flags on the Dolma Pass

Gompa of Milarepa

The walk

The walk

Chiu Gompa

Newly constructed Gompa, but no one is allowed to reside here.
Poor quality building hastens the deterioration

Lake Manasarovar

Where do we go, What future

Sheep Milking

The mess of Saga

Zhangmu

Padmasambhava

Nomad

Will she forget me

Last time for this horseman, he really doesn't want to go!!!

NEPAL
JUNE 14TH-JUNE 20TH

We walk headlong into the usual chaos that is Nepal. Some of the group are not sure if they have the appropriate re-entry visa and the officials don't seem to know either! The courteous nod and "Tashi deleh" that we have become used to is replaced with hostile looks and wolf whistles. A stream of Nepalese women carry the bags to the waiting coach—next stop Kathmandu.

Within twenty minutes it is clear we are being driven by a driver with a death wish. Ferris, seated behind me, is shouting for the coach to stop and he be let off. Ramesh's patience is wearing thin and a heated exchange follows. The coach driver is not interested in slowing; I think everyone just wants to get home to Kathmandu. The mountains, now on the left, continue to partner our journey. It is heartbreaking to sit and watch them knowing that on the other side is Tibet. We are continuously descending, and the landscape is changing. The beautifully terraced hillsides support a crop growing system that features in the highlands of Nepal but are badly in need of the rains, which apparently have not yet arrived. We stop for a photo of an amazing group of bee hives, suspended from the cliff face. Other than that, despite different complaints from Ferris, we keep going for the full six hour drive until the deteriorating air quality and the slums tell us we are nearly back in Kathmandu. The traffic disgorging plumes of toxic fumes, the noise and the filth are quite depressing. At 5pm we pull into the entrance of the Radisson Hotel. Rainy and I are allocated a room with no window ledge! and given two hours to reorganize and reassemble in the hotel lounge for celebration drinks and dinner. I leave her to it, needing the space of a walk.

The pollution is so bad after the mountains I return to the hotel after only ten minutes. The shower is warm and soothing, but it is proving very difficult to lift my heart. Ironically I felt similar when I saw Lhasa for the first time, now it is because I have left. Everyone looks as neat as a new pin, quite glamorous in fact. Ferris and Tenzin arrive and there is a silence. Tenzin has changed back into his Abbot's robes and his head freshly shaven. Obviously no one in the group knew his true identity. Saumya, despite her dark Sri Lankan complexion is clearly flushed.

"You look quite embarrassed." I remark.

"I told him to clench his buttocks, no one said he is a Buddhist monk".

"Actually he is a renowned Amchi Buddhist doctor and Abbot of his Monastery in Mustang." My comments make her feel worse! But we both see the funny side of what happened. Ferris and Tenzin take their leave as they do not wish to be part of the 'group Dinner'. Ramesh walks us through a maze of alleys to a local eatery, and judging by the number of Kailash trip paraphernalia that adorns the walls, this is the standard end to the tour. It doesn't go well. Heated exchanges between Susan and the others over the share bar bill leave me wondering why any of these people bothered to make pilgrimage. But they didn't. It was just a challenging hike, and they learned nothing. Behaviour patterns soon reassert themselves, the next tour has already been

booked by some, and life will go on as usual.

MONDAY JUNE 15TH

Checkout is to be completed by 10am. The front lobby is buzzing with farewells, email exchanges and the Army! We have woken to an all out general strike, including transport. Apart from Susan, Meryl and myself the others have to be at the airport for their flights home. The Army have been called in to provide transport. They leave the hotel with an armed guard both on and off the bus. I now have to consider where I am going and how. I have allowed five days downtime before returning to New Zealand, part of which I have a reservation in a village of Nagarkot, about 2 hours drive and situated with good views of the Langtang mountain range. For today I have to find somewhere in Kathmandu, and get myself and luggage out of The Radisson. Susan has recommended a guest house in Chettrapati, called the Himal Ganesh. Leaving the luggage with the doorman I head off on foot. The suburb of Chettrapati is about a three kilometre walk, and again in the budget end of town. I am pleasantly surprised when I do eventually find it. Two Tibetan sisters own and run this place, which is set down a side road, and quite peaceful. It has a pleasant garden and is only US$11 per night. The task of getting all my bags here is a problem. I return to the Radisson where the helpful doorman thinks he can find a cycle rickshaw that will help. Sure enough, within twenty minutes a cycle rickshaw arrives and loads up. We run into trouble as soon as we leave the hotel compound. We are confronted by several thugs, armed with crowbars, demanding that the ride be immediately stopped and the rickshaw return home. Despite my pleading, the tension overheats, I and my luggage are turned out and the crowbars start work on the passenger part of the rickshaw. The poor man shouts and pleads for them to stop, as I pick myself up, scrambling for some distance. It is a terrifying experience, and a wake up call to how bad things have got in Nepal. A more senior man arrives on the scene and after some discussion the attack is halted and the thugs withdraw up the road. The poor rickshaw driver is beside himself with fear, however he picks up my bags, reloads them on what is left of his livelihood and we are able, very slowly, to resume our journey on foot. He uses side streets and back alleys, it takes two hours to reach the Himal Ganesh. In the quiet of the garden and over a sweet lassi he tries to explain that all of the trouble is caused by the Maoists. The political turmoil is more acute than ever with a rebel Maoist army being left in the hills of Nepal unsure of what their role, if any, will be in a coalition Government. Most of the population would like to be able to get on with life, but live under the constant threat of scenes similar to today. Most rickshaw and taxi drivers have to pay protection money to the rebels, in order to be left alone. Apprehension about a two hour drive tomorrow settles in my mind. A decision best left until the morning when I can try to evaluate the situation more clearly. Certainly it is best to stay off the streets for the remainder of today.

TUESDAY JUNE 16TH

The strike seems to be over, but I do take the advice from the two sisters and arrange a taxi up to Nagarkot. The driver, another Ramesh, is happy to strike a fair price. Within twenty minutes of the journey we are stopped by crowbar-wielding thugs. I am beginning to wish I had got a flight back to New Zealand rather than stay in Nepal. Ramesh is clearly nervous and I see him give a bundle of Rupees, payment to be left alone. He explains this is an everyday occurrence and no one seems to be able to stop the intimidation and corruption.

As we get up into the hills, the air clears as does the tension. The views are magnificent, as we climb to an altitude of 3,200 metres. I have a reservation at the Country Club Villa, supposedly one of the better lodges, but as we approach the village I can see how neglected the whole place is. Hotels of a bygone era, some with turrets and huge grandiose facades, are in a state of decay. Stonework is crumbling, grounds are neglected. It is hard to believe that they still advertise for guests, but they do, most displaying a large vacancy sign! Thankfully the Country Club Villa Hotel is not in such a shocking state. However the room description, just as at the Utse Hotel in Kathmandu, is a far cry from reality. Again there are very few guests and most of the staff, if there are any, appears to have the day off. The hotel manager does oblige me with a pot of afternoon tea, served on the wide terrace. Had the mountains not been obscured by the heat haze and dust from

Kathmandu the view would have been spectacular. In the gardens below, I hear the call of peacocks, a lonely sound echoed by the sense of emptiness that hangs in the valley. Will this be a time for reflection of the last six weeks?

Later on in the evening the hotel is swamped by seventy two Indians on their way to do pilgrimage at Mount Kailash. I sit quietly at a corner table in the restaurant and listen to the build up of excitement that precludes their once in a lifetime dream; so many of them are very overweight and older in years. I wonder if any will meet the cremation pyre?

WEDNESDAY JUNE 17TH

I wake feeling absolutely terrible. My cough has returned, my limbs are swollen and bouts of nausea wash over me. The indefinable sense of tension returns, I think it better to return to Kathmandu as soon as possible. The hotel is deserted, again, so not even a cup of tea is available. The Indians have gone, I would have asked for a lift down the mountain to the main road had I been up earlier. A walk does bring me to a couple of supply stores, and a bus enquiry office. It seems there is only one bus every other day, tomorrow being one of those days. Failing that it is a nine kilometre walk down the mountain to the main Kathmandu road where buses are more frequent and taxis can be found. As I walk back to the hotel I see a minibus parked outside one of the other lodges. Nothing ventured, nothing gained; I go in to find the driver. As luck would have it, yet another group of Indians are bound for Kathmandu in about an hour. They are

very accommodating and I secure a seat even though this is a private hire vehicle. I have enough time to gather by bags, pay the hotel bill, which includes a flat refusal to pay for the night I no longer require. This place is nowhere near the expectation delivered by the various accounts I had read. The same hostility and abandoned feel, plus the fact I have been taken ill.

The Indian visitors refuse to accept any money for my ride back to the city, and two hours later I am dropped off in New Road about twenty minutes walk from the Himal Ganesh. I thank them for their kindness. Still feeling very unwell I make it back to the peace of the hotel and the sisters. They are a little surprised to see me, expecting that I would like Nagarkot enough to stay the intended two days. I retreat to my room, switch on the television to find I am watching Ladies Day at Ascot Races in England!

THURSDAY JUNE 18TH

I now have two days in hand before my flight back to New Zealand. Nepal is no longer a place in which to reflect or relax. Constant power cuts, the refuse situation still not resolved, thugs demanding money, and everyone I meet anxious to discuss the political situation. The Dream Gardens, which were closed before, are now on my agenda, especially as it within walking distance. There seems to be a heavy presence of armed police, complete with riot control body protection and shields—not a good sign. As I skirt the area of Thamel, I see bonfires in the street, roads cordoned off, and groups of young men wielding sticks and crow bars. Hurrying on to my destination, I pray it is open.

The Dream Gardens were once a private garden, being 6,895 square meters. After the demise of its owner, Kaiser Shumsher, it was taken over by the Government with the inevitable result that it was not managed and fell into neglect. The renovation has been financed by the Austrian Government, with stunning results. As I enter the wrought iron gates, it is like entering a different world. Gone is the mayhem of the streets, replaced with tranquil ponds and waterfalls; beautiful pavilions and pagodas very much in early European style. There is an amphitheatre, following Greek architecture, birdhouses and urns. The garden, trees and shrubs are exquisitely laid out and perfectly maintained. The high walls act as a barrier against the urban noise; one could almost forget that one is in the heart of Kathmandu. This is one of my favourite forms for photography. It is years and years since I was able to work with sites such as the Taj Mahal, the Red Fort and Borobudur. I find the brick and plaster Egyptian Sphinx one of the most interesting small pieces. She has the body of a lion and usually the head of a human or a ram. This one has lost her head and tail during the years of neglect which makes her warning of strangling those who cannot answer her unspoken riddle rather alarming. "What am I, Who are you, what truth do you see in my face?" The tea salon is located at the Basanta Pavilion. I take a table on the upper level and am in no hurry to leave. Maybe here I can find that space needed to think back over the events of the last forty two days. In the normal course of one's life, forty two days is a drop in the ocean. None of us usually do very much with such a small drop. Given the opportunity to realize one's destiny or dream, forty two days is a lifetime.

FRIDAY JUNE 19TH

Breakfast in the small quiet garden is a nice way to start my last day. It will be a day of last minute gift shopping, packing and farewells. I will not be particularly sad to say goodbye to Kathmandu. It has become a sad place, wrecked with political upheaval since the Royal Family were either assassinated or sent into exile. China has an ever increasing influence and presence and the Tibetan community have found themselves in a dangerous position, far from the safe haven that Nepal once offered. On the last morning of the tour, back at the Radisson, Ramesh had told me to return to the Tour Company desk before I left for New Zealand. He was going to try and get a letter of explanation over the expense of the horse, for insurance purposes. I have no idea if he has been successful, but have the time to cover the three kilometres to the Radisson and back.

The friendly doorman gives me a warm greeting, and I give him a brief account of the thrashing the rickshaw was subjected to. He is most apologetic and despairs of the current situation. As he opens the big doors I am surprised by his comment.

"It has been a pleasure knowing you, Madam. Safe journey back to New Zealand." We have had the odd little chat as I have entered and exited the hotel, and return his

kind comment:

"It has been nice talking with you also; I hope your girls pass their exams with good results"

Just as I go through he doors, he again surprises me with his words.

"You are one of only a very few that have taken the time to talk to me. I am not permitted to engage the guests in conversation, and most just wait for the door to be opened. Thank you for your interest in my family."

I offer my hand, which he accepts, and shakes warmly.

Ramesh has been true to his word. A letter is waiting for my collection. It is not sealed, so I have a peek at what is written.

"To whom it may concern.

This is to confirm Jane Comer, traveling with the Kailash tour, contracted a serious chest infection. I administered a course of antibiotics, and our location meant there was no option other than to hire the service of a horse and its owner to enable Ms Comer to be taken off Mount Kailash. Cost $250 U.S. Yours Dr. Ramesh, followed by the Tour Company stamp."

Since when was Ramesh a Doctor! I have to smile a little at the wording, with the slight tweak of the facts! I am doubtful if the insurance company is going to buy the idea of a horse, but I will submit it anyway when I get back. As I turn to leave, I notice the hotel bakery is open. During the two days, here at the beginning of the trip I had to bypass this temptation as it was simply far too expensive. Now on my last few hours and, with rupees to shed, I can indulge myself. I feel like one of the characters from the film 'Willy Wonkas Chocolate Factory'—where to start! The melt-in-the-mouth cheesecake just slides down without any effort—this is gorgeous!

The owners of the hotel invite me to have dinner with them, which I enjoy. I give each a *khata*; my way of expressing appreciation for the warmth they have shown me, even though I have only been a guest for a couple of days.

I sit out in the garden until late, thinking about the long trip home, when the hotel cat arrives for a chat.

SATURDAY JUNE 20TH. THE JOURNEY HOME

It does not get off to a good start, with nearly an hour's delay on the departure time. I have a connection in Singapore which allows only fifty minutes to disembark, change terminal and board the flight for New Zealand. On arrival at Changi Airport I run for the electric shuttle operating between terminals, with only twenty minutes remaining before the gate shuts for the New Zealand flight.

Somehow, I mishear the message about staying on this car or changing, depending on which terminal is required. I end up going back to where I started. Absolute panic as I restart the journey in disbelief about my stupid mistake. I arrive at the gate with only seconds to spare, and now face another challenge. The X-ray machine has picked up my bottle of water from Lake Manasarovar. There was not a hint of a problem exiting Nepal. "You can't take that, it is sacred water from a Lake in Tibet." I plead. "You cannot take this on board Madam, even if it is Holy water from Rome," is the curt reply. Well, there is only one thing left to do. I grab the bottle back, and drink the contents.

As the Islands of New Zealand come into view, I recall the moment the Roof of the World burst through the clouds. One day I shall go back and meet a young woman called Dolma, born 15th August 2009. She will talk of her father and the story he would tell her, of the English woman he escorted around the sacred mountain during one Saga Dawa. He knew they were old friends. I have touched this land, felt this land, and breathed this land. I have been born of this land, The Land of the Snows. Tibet.

VERSE FOR TIBET: Inspired by the lady in the café, Dharamsala.

> Through the hail and the thunder, I see all that's beyond,
> A glimmer of connection with a people so torn and confused.
> The lady just stares into a void of pain,
> I gather my thoughts, Lhasa Valley we see,
> Plains wide and serene.

We bathe for a while in this world that has been
Until the weather subsides,
A wave goodbye, all that we need.
I have been to our valley, not so green or serene
As we saw in those dreams.
Barren and harsh with the work of a demon,
senseless intrusion in a land that once teemed with nomads and yaks,
The gurs and the billy-goats now rarely seen.
The peaks now conceal great armies in red,
A land crying out for it's voice to be heard by the rest of the world.
FREE TIBET

FOR TASHI, WHOSE VOICE IS SILENCED

EPILOGUE

Some weeks after my return to New Zealand, I applied to the insurance company for a claim form. Finding the section marked 'Emergency Transport' I skipped past, rental car, bus, taxi, train, aircraft and reached any other. The box duly ticked, I now needed to submit a brief explanation of what other. Simple answer: A HORSE. Amazingly, I received a cheque two weeks later!

At the end of 2009 His Holiness The Dalai Lama did return to New Zealand to give two days teachings. The 'Friends of Tibet NZ' organise these visits and were most interested in the photographs I had taken. After much deliberation and work formatting them into a cohesive slide show, 73 were chosen to run on the big screens, either side of the stage in the Vector Arena, Auckland. Unfortunately on the day not only did the slide show not work, but the voice recording of His Holiness also failed. It was an honour though to have them chosen for such an enormous occasion. I also kept my word to Tashi, by including his simple request to His Holiness along with a khata from Lhasa, a photo of Kailash and a small packet containing the red earth, Dronkpa, from the mountain. I do not know if these things were given to him—maybe one day I will find out.

Published in the memory of the Tibetan Nun, Palden Choetso, who burned herself to death; November 3rd 2011; in protest against Chinese repression of Tibetans, in Tibet.

For the 24 Tibetans who have now burned themselves to death.

>Your prayers seem slow to ripen,
>But the fields of ears do hear,
>The warrior of change is riding
>windhorse, great Garuda,
>Repressions end is near.
>The aggressors face so clearly lit,
>By fiery torches on hillsides stand
>These withering blooms never lost from sight,
>Gesar's flower in their hands.

GLOSSARY

BARDO—The transitionary period between death and rebirth.

BODHISATTVA—A practioner who has reached enlightenment for the benefit of all sentient beings.

BÖN—The pre-Buddhist religion of Tibet, aspects of which have been adopted into Tibetan Buddhism.

BUDDHA—The awakened or Enlightened One. Denotes a state of mind.

CHENREZIG—The Tibetan name for **Avalokiteshvara**. The embodiment of infinite compassion. OM MANI PADME HUM is his six lettered mantra recited by all Buddhist practioners.

CHUBA—Tibetan tunic, worn by both men and women.

DALAI LAMA—Ocean of Wisdom. The spiritual and temporal leader of the Tibetan people.

DHARMA—The Buddha's teachings.

DORJE—Tibetan name for **Vajra**. The Thunderbolt or Sacred Sceptre used in Tantric rituals, cutting through ignorance and representing the indestructible nature of Buddhahood.

GAU—A locket, varying in size, to hold small symbols of protection for the wearer.

GAUTAMA BUDDHA—The original name for Shakyamuni Buddha.

GOMPA—A small village monastery.

HINAYANA BUDDHISM—"The Lower Vehicle" The path of the Shravakas, or Hearers, and Pratyeka Buddhas, or solitary realisers. Those who follow a path of self liberation with out the motivation of ending suffering for all sentient beings.

KARMA—The law of cause and effect.

KARMAPA—The head of the Kagyu lineage and wearer of the Black Crown.

KASHAG—The Tibetan Government in exile.

KHATA—White silk scarf given as an offering of respect and peace.

KHORA—The cicumbulation of a sacred site or building. Usually repeated 3 times in a clockwise direction.

MAHAMUDRA—"The Great Seal". A meditation technique employed to understand the relationship between the mind and the true nature of reality.

MAHAYANA BUDDHISM—"The Great Vehicle." Follows The Middle Way approach using practice and Bodhicitta to accumulate merit, leading to enlightenment or Nirvana. This may take eons.

MAITREYA BUDDHA—Jampa Chenmo is the Tibetan name. The future Buddha.

MALA BEADS—The Tibetan Rosary of 108 beads

MANTRA—A ritual formula of prayers and offerings associated with Tantric Buddhism.

MANI STONES—Tibet is littered with these. The six-lettered Mantra of Chenrezig is carved or painted onto any stone and left as an offering.

MANI PILLS—Made from yak butter and barley flour, coloured red. Symbolises taking Chenrezig, "The Great Compassionate One" into one's own body. Blessed by a Lama, Rinpoche, or Dalai lama.

MANJUSHRI—Embodiment of Wisdom cutting through misconception with his sword. He is a dominant figure in spreading the Dharma through Tibet.

MUDRA—Symbolic hand gestures.

NAMGYALMA—The Victorious One.

NIRVANA—Enlightenment. Free from Samsara and suffering, finding Dewachen, land of Pure Bliss.

PADMASAMBHAVA—Or **GURU RINPOCHE**. The Precious Master. Founder of the Nyingma Lineage, and cherished by Tibetans as the One who introduced Vajrayana Buddhism into Tibet. Thought to be an emanation of Amitabha, Buddha of Limitless Light.

PANCHEN LAMA—Head of Shigatse Monastery and next in importance to The Dalai

Lama. Instumental in the search for the reincarnation of Dalai Lamas after their death.

RINPOCHE—"The Precious One" A Title given to Buddhist Masters.

SAMSARA—Cyclic existence and source of all suffering. Continuous rebirth, sickness, aging and death.

SANGHA—The Monastic community.

SHAKYAMUNI BUDDHA—The present Buddha.

TARA—The Mother of all Buddhas.

THANGKA—Scroll painting of sacred images, usually on cloth or silk.

TSAMPA—Staple diet of Tibetans. Made from barley flour and water.

TUSHITA—Place of Joy. Offers courses for those new to Buddhism.

VAJRAPANI—The Diamond Holder, or Power Buddha.

VAJRAYANA BUDDHISM—The Diamond Vehicle. Tantric Buddhist practice involving deity meditation, and the most widely practiced in Tibet. Allows the practitioner to attain enlightenment in one lifetime.

VISPASSANA—Translates to "see things as they really are." Meditation focusing on the breath, and forming a connection between mind and body. Independent of any religious doctrine.

BIBLIOGRAPHY
Further reading on Tibet & Buddhism

Allen, Charles—A Mountain in Tibet

Dalai Lama of Tibet, The—My Land & My People

David-Neel, Alexandra—Magic & Mystery in Tibet

David-Neel, Alexandra—My Journey to Lhasa

Evans-Wentz, W.Y. (editor)—The Tibetan Book of the Great Liberation

Evans-Wentz, W.Y.—Tibet's Great Yogi Milarepa

Fleming, Peter—Bayonets to Lhasa

French, Patrick—Tibet, Tibet

Gyatso, Palden—Fire under the Snow: Testimony of a Tibetan Prisoner

Harrer, Heinrich—Seven Years in Tibet

Hopkirk, Peter—Trespassers on the Roof of the World

Huc, Abbé Evariste—Travels in Tartary & Thibet

Kawaguchi, Ekai—Three Years in Tibet

MacGregor, John—Tibet—a Chronicle of Exploration

Milarepa—Drinking the Mountain Stream (Songs of Tibet's Beloved Saint)

Norbu, Jamyang—Horseman in the Snow

Norbu, Thubten Jigme & Colin Turnbull—Tibet

Powers, John—A Concise Introduction to Tibetan Buddhism

Seth, Vikram—From Heaven Lake

CPSIA information can be obtained
at www.ICGtesting.com
Printed in the USA
LVIW010759130512

5161LVAU00001B

9781469157924